The Parables of the Kingdom

The Parables
of the Kingdom

by
John MacArthur, Jr.

MOODY PRESS
CHICAGO

© 1984, 1985 by
JOHN F. MACARTHUR, JR.

All rights reserved. No part of this book may be reproduced in any form without permission in writing from the publisher, except in the case of brief quotations embodied in critical articles or reviews.

All Scripture quotations, unless otherwise noted, are from the *New Scofield Reference Bible*, King James Version, © 1967 by Oxford University Press, Inc. Reprinted by permission.

ISBN: 0-8024-5112-8

1 2 3 4 5 6 7 Printing/GB/Year 90 89 88 87 86 85

Printed in the United States of America

Contents

CHAPTER	PAGE
1. Kingdom Parables—Part 1 Tape GC 2297—Matt. 13:1-2	1
2. Kingdom Parables—Part 2 Tape GC 2298—Matt. 13:3*a*, 10-17, 34, 35	16
3. The Responses to the Gospel Tape GC 2299—Matt. 13:3*b*-9, 18-23	32
4. The Kingdom and the World Tape GC 2300—Matt. 13:24-30, 36-43	50
5. The Power and Influence of Christ's Kingdom—Part 1 Tape GC 2301—Matt. 13:31-32	67
6. The Power and Influence of Christ's Kingdom—Part 2 Tape GC 2302—Matt. 13:33	82
7. Entering the Kingdom Tape GC 2303—Matt. 13:44-46	99
8. The Furnace of Fire Tape GC 2304—Matt. 13:47-52	115
Scripture Index	130

Matthew 13:1-2   Tape GC 2297

1
Kingdom Parables—Part 1

Outline

Introduction
- A. The King
  1. Depicted
  2. Denied
     - *a)* The inherent consequence
     - *b)* The illogical conclusion
- B. The Kingdom
  1. The postponement
  2. The promise
  3. The parenthesis
     - *a)* The circumstance
       - (1) Explained
       - (2) Exemplified
     - *b)* The concept
       - (1) Universal kingdom
         - (*a*) Psalm 29:10
         - (*b*) Psalm 103:19
         - (*c*) 1 Chronicles 29:11
       - (2) Mediatorial kingdom
         - (*a*) In the Old Testament
         - (*b*) In the New Testament
     - *c)* The composition
       - (1) Matthew 8:12
       - (2) John 15:2, 6
     - *d)* The conditions
       - (1) The internal kingdom offered
       - (2) The external kingdom observed
     - *e)* The clarifications
       - (1) The kingdom of heaven
       - (2) The church age

Lesson
- I. The place
  - A. The Duration of Ministry Continued
  - B. The Dimension of Ministry Changed
    1. A change of territory

2. A change in teaching
      a) The interest of the people
      b) The initiation of the parables

Introduction

A. The King
   1. Depicted

      The book of Matthew was written primarily to present Jesus Christ as the King, the Son of God, the Messiah, and the rightful heir to David's throne. In chapter 1, Matthew shows that He is the One who should reign because He is in the messianic line. He is the Son of David. In chapter 2, His right to reign is affirmed by the oriental king-makers that we know as the wise men, or the magi. Through their own understanding of prophecy and the direction of the Spirit of God, they are led to confirm that Jesus is the King. Christ's kingship is affirmed again in chapter 3 by the testimony of John the Baptist, who was the preordained forerunner to the King. In chapter 4, Christ is presented as God's chosen King by His conflict with Satan: He overpowers Satan and conquers the kingdom of darkness.

      In chapters 5, 6, and 7, Jesus speaks with authority—He speaks as a King. Here, He talks about the principles of the kingdom. Those chapters make up the great Sermon on the Mount. Chapters 8-10 present the credentials of the King. Those three chapters are full of miracles, which are all proof that he fulfilled the prophecies concerning Him. He proved Himself to be the King through His supernatural power.

   2. Denied

      In chapters 8-10, while Christ is performing His miracles, there is a mounting rejection of Him. The greater the evidence that He is the King, the greater the rejection becomes. That shows the profound blindness of the people. In chapter 11, Jesus denounces the sinful nation of Israel for rejecting Him. He promises them severe judgment. Then chapter 11 closes with His invitation: "Come unto me, all ye that labor and are heavy laden, and I will give you rest" (v. 28). Out of the message of judgment comes the message of grace—an invitation. In chapter 12, that rejection reaches its climax as does the pronouncement of judgment. The final rejection by the leaders of Israel is summed up in the fact that Jesus is accused of being satanic. Jesus then pronounces a final judgment on the leaders and says, "You're beyond the point of being forgiven" (vv. 31-32). But even after saying that, Jesus closes with another invitation:

"For whosoever shall do the will of my Father, who is in heaven, the same is my brother, and sister, and mother" (v. 50). What is the will of the Father in heaven? Very clearly the Father had said, "This is my beloved Son, in whom I am well pleased; hear ye him" (Matt. 17:5*b*).Whoever recognizes Jesus as the Son of God and hears His message, will come into an intimate relationship with Jesus Christ.

    a) The inherent consequence

        Christ had been proved to be the King. The people had rejected Him as the King, and consequently, He pronounced judgment on them. Yet He still offers an invitation to whomever will believe. So as we approach chapter 13, the die is cast. Israel had rejected the King. Therefore, Israel had rejected the kingdom, because the kingdom cannot be separated from the King. For centuries, they had awaited the Messiah and His establishment of God's kingdom on earth. They had awaited the restoration of the glory and the blessing that was man's before the fall. But when it was offered to them, they refused it and therefore lost it in that generation.

    b) The illogical conclusion

        Starting with chapter 13, we enter a new perspective in the ministry of Christ. Stanley Toussaint, in his commentary on Matthew, says, "Not seeing the Messiahship of Jesus in His words and works, they have separated the fruit from the tree" (*Behold the King* [Portland: Multnomah, 1980], p. 168). I think that is an important statement. The Jewish leaders came to the wrong conclusion about Jesus not because they denied His power or weren't fascinated by His words, but because they never traced the fruit of Christ's ministry to its logical conclusion. They separated it from the reality of who He was. You can see in chapter 13 the shadow of the cross looming in the background. They were already seeking to destroy Him in Matthew 12:14. They had reached the point of wanting only to kill Him. They had rejected the King and His kingdom.

B. The Kingdom

  1. The postponement

    Now, the question that immediately comes to mind is this: If Jesus came to bring His kingdom to earth, to regin and to establish that which was promised, but Israel refused Him and His kingdom, then what happened to the kingdom? Chapter 13 answers that question. You see, the kingdom cannot come until the nation of Israel receives the King. Until that point, then, the kingdom has to be postponed in terms of its complete fulfillment. It has to be postponed to a future time. What time is that? The second coming of Christ. That's why Christ is coming a second time—to bring the kingdom that was refused at His first coming. Christ came and said, "Repent; for the kingdom of heaven is at hand" (Matt. 4:17). The message of John the Baptist and the apostles was the same (Matt. 3:2; 10:7). They preached that the kingdom of God was at hand. But the people rejected the King and His kingdom; therefore, the kingdom was postponed.

2. The promise

You say, "Why didn't God just eliminate the kingdom altogether?" Because God promised Israel a future kingdom, and God keeps His promises. That's why Christ is coming back to offer His kingdom again, and at that time it will be received. God promised that He would bring a kingdom to Israel and that through that nation His kingdom would extend to all the world. God will keep His promise. That's why the Jewish people are still on the earth right now and they are regathered in their land. God's plan is right on target for them. If God just set the kingdom aside and said, "Forget it; I gave you one chance at it," then His prophecies would not come to pass and His word would be violated. Thus, God postponed the kingdom to a time when Israel will believe.

Zechariah 12:10 says that there is coming a day when Israel shall "look upon [Him] whom they have pierced, and they shall mourn for him, as one mourneth for his only son." Then Zechariah 13:1 adds that a fountain of salvation will be opened up to the line of Israel, and the nation will be regenerated. They will be redeemed. Paul said in Romans 11:26 that "all Israel shall be saved." That will happen during the Great Tribulation. Revelation 7:9 says that there will also be a multitude of Gentiles saved during that time. There will be people of every tongue, tribe, and nation in that multitude. When the kingdom of God comes into the the hearts of men internally, then its complete fulfillment will come externally, when Christ reigns on the earth in the Millennium (the thousand-year reign of Christ spoken of in Revelation 20). The complete fulfillment of the kingdom refers to the kingdom that will be on the earth both internally (in the hearts of believing people) and externally (as Christ reigns as King).

Had the Jewish people believed Christ the first time He came, they would have received the King internally and the kingdom externally. But because they didn't believe, the complete fulfillment of the kingdom was postponed. There was a remnant who received the King internally, and today there are those who receive the King internally, but someday there will be a massive response to Him. When the kingdom comes internally at the level that it does in the Tribulation, then it will come externally in the wonderful millennial reign.

3. The parenthesis

Now, what happens in the time between the rejection of the kingdom and Christ's second coming? Some theologians have called this period "the parenthesis," some have called it "the interim," and some have called it "the interregnum." It is a period that is not seen in the Old Testament. Thus Jesus calls it "the mystery" in Mark 4:11. It was a period of time hidden from the people. That's why chapter 13 is so essential, because there were no teachings on what that period of time would be like. Throughout chapter 13 are seven parables, and it is in those parables that Jesus describes the interim period.

We are living in that period now. If we can understand what Jesus says about that period, then we can know what we should be doing during it. That is why we need to understand chapter 13. As we study the parables, you'll see the perfect parallel they have to our time.

That time is also known as the mystery form of the kingdom. That doesn't mean it is clandestine or secretive; it just means that it was hidden and is now revealed. The Old Testament people thought that the Messiah would set up His kingdom right after He came to earth. There were a few subtle hints given to them about the interim period, but there was never a full description of it.

a) The circumstance

(1) Explained

During the interim period, the kingdom goes on while the King is absent. Jesus, at that point, is in heaven. That doesn't mean He's not present in our midst, for the Bible says that He is. But in His glorified body, He dwells at the right hand of the Father. It is there that He intercedes for us to the Father, and awaits the time of His second coming. So, there's a sense in which the kingdom is here on earth while the King is in absentia. Some theologians have difficulty with that and say you can't have a kingdom if the King isn't here. That is not true. There is a realm here, and in this realm there are people who are subjects of Christ. Jesus is the King by definition of who He is, even though He is in absentia.

(2) Exemplified

A classic illustration that proves this possible is found in 2 Samuel 15-17. David was still the king of Israel even though his son Absalom usurped him and Absalom's revolutionary cohorts rejected him. It didn't matter that they chased him into the wilderness and that he hid for a long period of time to avoid being killed. He was still the king, and Israel was still his realm. He still had the right to rule and was the recognized monarch in the hearts of many of the people. Eventually, He was able to come back to take up the throne that was rightfully his. In the same way that David was king in absentia during that incident, Christ is King now.

) The concept

The Lord Jesus Christ is ruling on the earth now even though He Himself in His glorified form is absent. To help you understand that better, I want to explain the concept of the kingdom. It is a very big issue to discuss, but we'll discuss it in reduced form and look at the heart of the matter.

There are two basic aspects of God's kingdom. The first aspect is God's:

(1) Universal kingdom

This simply refers to the fact that God rules everything and everyone forever. He is the Sovereign, the Creator, the Sustainer, the beginning and the end of all things, and He dominates all things.

(*a*) Psalm 29:10—"The Lord sitteth upon the flood; yea, the Lord sitteth King forever." He is the eternal King. There is no time when He is not the King and there is no time when someone else takes His place.

(*b*) Psalm 103:19—"The Lord hath prepared His throne in the heavens, and his kingdom ruleth over all." He is the King over everything. You say, "Is He King over the devil?" Not only is He King over the devil, but He's also King over the demons and unbelievers. That's why He has the power to throw them all into hell. The Bible says to "fear him who is able to destroy both soul and body in hell" (Matt. 10:28). Hell is not controlled by Satan. God will punish Satan in hell along with the demons and unbelievers. God rules over hell just like He rules over everything else in His universal monarchy.

(*c*) 1 Chronicles 29:11—"Thine, O Lord, is the greatness, and the power, and the glory, and the victory, and the majesty; for all that is in the heaven and in the earth is thine. Thine is the kingdom, O Lord, and thou art exalted as head above all."

God is the universal King. Sometimes when you read the phrase "the kingdom of God" in the Bible, it refers to God's universal rule.

The second aspect of God's kingdom is the:

(2) Mediatorial kingdom

I have searched for a better definition of this aspect of God's kingdom and can't find one. Alva McClain calls it "the mediatorial Kingdom" (*The Greatness of the Kingdom: An Inductive Study of the Kingdom of God as Set Forth in the Scriptures* [Grand Rapids: Zondervan, 1959]). In other words, it is not the direct rule of God. but His rule mediated through human instruments. That refers to God's rule on earth. It is the kingdom that the Lord had in mind when He said, "After this manner, therefore, pray ye. . . . Thy kingdom come. Thy will be done in earth, as it is in heaven" (Matt. 6:9a, 10). The phrase "as it is in heaven" perceives the universal kingdom of God, and the phrase "in earth" perceives the earthly, mediated kingdom of God. We are to pray, "God, rule on the earth the way You rule everywhere else." That isolates the earth as a point of rebellion in the midst of God's universal kingdom. When God created the world, He planned to rule on the earth through human instruments. The first two people He ruled through were Adam and Eve. He gave them dominion over the Earth (Gen. 1:28). He told them to rule for Him; He made them His vice-monarchs.

When Adam and Eve fell prey to Satan, rebellion set in, and Satan became the monarch of this world. There is now ruling on the earth a usurper. But God said, "I still want to mediate My rule on the earth. I want My will and My Word known. I want my moral standards known and people to be subject to Me. I want to call men into my kingdom." He is doing just that and has been ever since the Fall.

(a) In the Old Testament

If you read the book of Genesis, you'll see that God mediated His rule on the earth through the patriarchs. The patriarchs were men who knew the mind, heart, and will of God. They had expressed God's will, heart, and mind to the people of their time. God mediated His rule through Seth, Noah, Abraham, Isaac, Jacob, Joseph, Melchizedek (who was priest of God), and other such individuals.

Later on, God called out a nation of people to be the human agents of His mediatorial kingdom. That nation was Israel, and they were to give the Word of God, the mind of God, and the heart of God to the world and to bring the world to know God (Deut. 6:4-7; cf. Gen. 12:2-3; Isa. 43:10, 12). Throughout the Old Testament God called prophets, priests, and kings to be His key human instruments in mediating His rule on earth.

(*b*) In the New Testament

God became directly involved in mediating His kingdom through the human instrument Jesus Christ. Jesus came into this world and told us what God was like and what His standards were. He preached about the kingdom of God and called for people to be subject to it.

After Jesus was rejected, He went back into heaven and the message was carried on by the apostles and prophets. God now mediates His rule on earth through the church, which is made up of believers who are indwelt by the Holy Spirit. As God's agents, we are to speak the Word of God; hold up the standards of God; bring God's will, way, and moral values to men; and call men to enter into God's kingdom.

There is coming a time in the future, during the Tribulation, when God will anoint 144,000 Jewish people to mediate His rule and take His message to the world. There will be a worldwide revival in which numerous Gentiles and Jewish people are saved, and then Christ will come back and mediate His own kingdom on the earth again. That mediated kingdom will eventually merge into the eternal kingdom, which will have "a new heaven and a new earth" (Rev. 21:1). The mediatorial kingdom, which began at creation, will end at that final merger, and we'll go into eternity that way.

c) The composition

Let me share with you something of interest about the mediatorial kingdom. It is a kingdom composed of those who are true to God and those who are falsely attached to God. The term *mediatorial kingdom* encompasses everyone who externally identifies himself with the people of God. This kingdom is made up of people who outwardly profess to be Christians (but aren't really Christians) and people who inwardly possess Christ. Oftentimes, we cannot tell who is really a Chrstian and who isn't.

That has been true of God's mediatorial kingdom ever since the Fall. When God was mediating His kingdom through the nation of Israel, there were some people who weren't really true to Him. In Romans 9 Paul writes, "For they are not all Israel, who are of Israel" (v. 6*b*). In Romans 2 he says, "For [a Jew] is not a Jew who is one outwardly . . . but he is a Jew who is one inwardly" (vv. 28*a*, 29*a*). There will always be people who identify themselves with God, whether they are really with Him or not.

Let me give you two illustrations of this.

(1) Matthew 8:12

Here we read, "But the sons of the kingdom shall be cast out into outer darkness; there shall be weeping and gnashing of teeth." That is a description of hell. Now, those who are believers do not go to hell. It is only unbelievers who go to hell. Notice the title used for those who will be cast into hell—"the sons of the kingdom." Because believers do not go to hell, we can conclude that not all sons of the kingdom are believers. The Lord Himself makes that clear here.

Within the framework of the kingdom are the true and the false. We'll see that in Matthew 13 in the parable of the tares among the wheat.

(2) John 15:2, 6

People sometimes become confused about John 15 because they don't understand that the concept of the mediatorial kingdom encompasses the true and the false. John 15 does not use the kingdom metaphor; it uses the concept of a vine and its branches, which is an agricultural metaphor. In this concept, Jesus is the vine. Who are the branches? Look at verse 2: "Every branch in me." The branches are people who somehow are connected with Christ. Jesus said, "Every branch in me that beareth not fruit he [God] taketh away." What happens to the branches that are taken away? Verse 6 tells us: "Men gather them, and cast them into the fire, and they are burned." That describes hell. A branch that doesn't bear fruit is going to be thrown into hell.

You say, "Wait a minute! Does that mean you can lose your salvation?" No, it doesn't. It is merely speaking of the fact that you can be in the kingdom and not of the King. You can be superficially attached. I think he's talking about a Judas branch here. The outward attachment is there, but the obvious lack of life is manifest by the fact that there is no fruit. You will need to keep that principle in mind as we study Matthew 13. Some of the "sons of the kingdom"—some of the branches—are going to go to hell because there was no real life in them. There was no real subjection to the King. Let me give you another thought about the interim period in which we live.

d) The conditions

God's universal kingdom has no conditions for entrance. In other words, everybody and everything is already under God's universal rule. But God's mediatorial kingdom has a condition—you're not really in His mediated kingdom unless, according to Mark 1:15, you "repent, and believe the gospel." If you don't do that, then you aren't truly in God's mediated kingdom, but you're still in His universal kingdom. You will suffer under His universal rule over hell and not know the blessing of heaven.

(1) The internal kingdom offered

When Jesus says in Matthew 4:17, "Repent; for the kingdom of heaven is at hand," what is He asking men to come into? He was inviting them into the mediatorial aspect of His kingdom—the redeemed community. There is no room for a neutral response here. The Lord repeatedly said, "You either receive Me or you don't" (Matt. 12:30; Mark 9:40). You either accept the King or reject Him and therefore either enter the kingdom or are kept out.

John the Baptist asked the Jewish people to make a decision, too. Tragically, they made the wrong decision. They refused the King and therefore refused His kingdom. Because of their rejection, judgment was pronounced on them. At that point, the complete fulfillment of the kingdom was postponed. You say, "Does that mean there is no kingdom now?" No, the kingdom does exist now, but it is an internal kingdom. In its complete fulfillment, it will be both internal and external.

(2) The external kingdom observed

The Scripture talks about a day when Jesus Christ will be sitting on the throne of David in the literal city of Jerusalem as He rules with a rod of iron and is sought by the nations (Ps. 2:6-9; Isa. 9:7; 11:1-5, 10). That will be the real, external kingdom of Christ. In Revelation 20, we read that the kingdom (the millennial kingdom) will be on earth for a thousand years. It will be preceded by an internal response to Christ on a worldwide basis. For now, the external element of the kingdom, or the fullness of the kingdom, awaits the belief of Israel. In the meantime, the kingdom is internal and God is reaching out across the world and bringing people into His kingdom through salvation.

e) The clarifications

(1) The kingdom of heaven

I would like to bring to your attention something of importance at this introductory level of our study. In Matthew 13:11, Jesus said, "It is given unto you to know the mysteries [the mystery form] of the kingdom of heaven." The phrase "the kingdom of heaven" is very important in this chapter and appears eight times (vv. 11, 24, 31, 33, 44, 45, 47, 52).

Some people have tried to suggest that the kingdom of heaven and the kingdom of God are two different things. That is not true. The kingdom of heaven is simply another way of saying the kingdom of God. The reason we know that is because in Luke 8:10, a parallel passage of Matthew 13:11, "the kingdom of God" is used instead of "the kingdom of heaven." Thus, we accept the fact that the kingdom of God and the kingdom of heaven are the same.

(2) The church age

The interim period we live in is also called the church age. We are in the unique mystery period that is defined by the apostle Paul in Ephesians 3: "[This is the mystery] which in other ages was not made known unto the sons of men, as it is now revealed unto his holy apostles and prophets by the Spirit: that the Gentiles should be fellow heirs, and of the same body, and partakers of his promise in Christ by the gospel" (vv. 5-6). In other words, the mystery of this age is that both Jew and Gentile would constitute a new body, or a new identity. That new identity is the church, and the church is the Body of Christ. That was not seen in the Old Testament. So there is a sense in which this age is the mystery age, the kingdom, and the church age. The kingdom, however, is not the same as the church. The kingdom was here before the church and it goes on beyond the church. It is just for this period of time that they are the same.

I might add that within the mediatorial kingdom there will always be the true and false. That was true in the

Old Testament nation of Israel. It is true now in the church. It will even be true in the Millennium. There will be believers and unbelievers on the earth during the reign of Christ. That is shown by the fact that when Satan is loosed from the pit at the end of Christ's one-thousand-year reign, he will go about the earth, gather a multitude of people, and make an army of them to fight against Christ (Rev. 20:7-9). Whatever aspect of the mediated kingdom you look at—the Old Testament, the Millennium, or the time in between—you will always see the true and the false side by side. That's why we shouldn't be surprised to find unbelieving people associated with the church.

Now, there are four things that I want to focus on in an overview of Matthew 13: The Place, The Plan, The Purpose, and The Promise.

Lesson

I. THE PLACE (vv. 1-2)

   A. The Duration of Ministry Continued

   Verse 1 starts by saying, "The same day." What does that mean? It simply means that what follows that phrase occurred on the same day as what happened in the preceding verses. In 12:46 we are told that Jesus is in a house and that His mother and brothers come to speak with Him. Prior to that, He had condemned the Pharisees, who had earlier accused Him of blasphemy. In 12:22 He had healed a demon-possessed man who was blind and dumb (and perhaps deaf). It's possible that on the same day He did other healings. He healed a demoniac, He was blasphemed, He pronounced judgment on the Pharisees, His parents and brothers came to Him, and He gave an invitation for people to do the will of the Father—all in one day! It had been a busy day for Him.

   B. The Dimension of Ministry Changed

   1. A change of territory

   Reading all of verse 1, it says, "The same day went Jesus out of the house, and sat by the seaside." This verse doesn't convey any profound spiritual truth, so why is it important to mention? Matthew could have started at verse 3: "He spoke many things unto them in parables." Verses 1 and 2 just say, "The same day went Jesus out of the house, and sat by the seaside. And great multitudes were gathered together unto him, so that he went into a boat, and sat; and the whole multitude stood on the shore." Was it necessary to include that information?

   It's interesting to note that at the beginning of Jesus' ministry, He was in houses a lot. From here on, however, toward the end of His ministry, He seems to be outdoors a lot. You see Him teaching by the seaside, on the highways and byways, in the village streets, on the hillsides, and in the countryside. It's almost as if Jesus' ministry was going into a new dimension. Another noticeable change is that in the latter part of His ministry, Jesus spent less time in the synagogues. The times He did go into a synagogue, He faced extreme hostility.

2. A change in teaching

   a) The interest of the people

   Verse 2 says that there was a great multitude around Him. It was an indiscriminate multitude. Public curiosity about Jesus was still very high. In spite of the rejection of the Jewish leaders, there were many people who were interested in Him. He fascinated people. In verse 2, there was such a big mob around Him that they practically pushed Him into the water. Imagine the pressure that must have been on Jesus! With all of the healings that He did and the words that He spoke, He became the attraction of attractions. There weren't books and other sources of entertainment available in those days. The things that Jesus was doing fascinated many people.

   Because of the pressing crowd, Jesus got one of the little fishing boats that was beached on the sand, and, probably with the help of the twelve (or some of the twelve), He pushed the boat out into the water. Then He got into the boat. The men helping Him probably stopped when they stood waist deep in the water, holding onto the boat to keep it from spinning around or being carried along by the tide. Then He sat in the boat. I once read a book that connected that action with the fact that rabbis always sat when they taught, but I think the reason He sat was because if He hadn't, He would've fallen in the water. It is a lot easier to sit in a boat than stand in it while it is bouncing back and forth in the tide.

   b) The initiation of the parables

   While the multitude stood on the shore, "He spoke many things unto them in parables" (v. 3*a*). Before that time, whenever Jesus taught he spoke in clear terms. However, many people had refused to listen to Him. So he began to teach parables that weren't able to be understood. Before that point, there is no record of Jesus having spoken in parables. He gave some wonderful allusions and figures of speech, but no parables. A parable, when it is left unexplained, is a riddle that cannot be understood. When the people refused to listen to what they could have understood, Jesus began to speak in riddles that they couldn't understand. First Corinthians 14:21 refers to the fact that the Lord would speak in a language that couldn't be understood to those who didn't listen to Him. Jesus' speaking in parables marked a turning point in His ministry. But to those who believed, He explained every single detail of what He said.

Focusing on the Facts

1. For what primary purpose was the book of Matthew written? How does Matthew prove that Jesus is King in the chapters preceding chapter 13 (see p. 2)?
2. What was the consequence of Israel's rejection of the King (see p. 3)?
3. Explain what Stanley Toussaint meant by the phrase "they [the Israelites] have separated the fruit from the tree" (see p. 3).
4. Why was the kingdom postponed? When will the kingdom come (see pp. 3-4)?
5. What would happen if God eliminated the kingdom altogether (see p. 4)?
6. Will the Jewish people eventually accept Christ as their Messiah? Support your explanation with Scripture (see p. 4).
7. What are the different titles that have been given to the time period between the rejection of the kingdom and Christ's second coming? Why did Jesus call that period of time "the mystery" (Mark 4:11)? What does Jesus describe in Matthew 13 (see p. 5)?
8. During the interim period, the _____ goes on with the King being _____. Give an illustration of that from the Old Testament (see pp. 5-6).
9. Define what is meant by the term *universal kingdom*. Does God extend His universal rule over Satan? Explain (see p. 6).
10. Define what is meant by the term *mediatorial kingdom*. How did God mediate His rule in the Old Testament era? How did God mediate His rule in the New Testament era? How does God mediate His rule now (see pp. 7-8)?
11. How will God mediate His rule during the Tribulation? After the Tribulation, Christ will come back to earth to mediate His rule again. What will the mediated kingdom eventually merge into (see p. 8)?
12. From the human point of view, what two kinds of people are in the mediatorial kingdom? Are all "the sons of the kingdom" believers (Matt. 8:12)? Explain (see pp. 8-9).
13. What will God do with branches that do not bear fruit (John 15:2, 6)? Does that mean you can lose your salvation? Explain (see p. 9).
14. Which aspect of God's kingdom is everyone in? What is the condition for *truly* becoming a part of God's mediatorial kingdom? (see p. 10)?

15. How do we know that the kingdom of heaven and the kingdom of God are the same (see p. 11)?
16. What is another term used for the interim period we live in now? What is the mystery of this age, according to Ephesians 3:5-6 (see p. 11)?
17. Is the kingdom the same as the church? Why (see p. 11)?
18. How do we know that there will be unbelievers on the earth during Christ's millennial reign? What Scripture supports that (see p. 12)?
19. What is the meaning of the phrase, "the same day" in Matthew 13:1? What happened during that day (see p. 12)?
20. How was the latter part of Jesus' ministry different from the earlier part (see pp. 12-13)?
21. Explain the difference between how Jesus taught prior to Matthew 13 and how He taught afterwards. What is a parable? Who were the only people Jesus explained His parables to (see pp. 13-14)?

Pondering the Principles

1. When the Jewish people rejected Jesus as their King, they also rejected the kingdom that God had repeatedly promised He would give them. Despite their rejection, God is still holding to His promise that Israel will one day have a kingdom ruled by their Messiah. One of the most wonderful things about God is that we can always be sure He will keep His promises. Read the following verses: Psalm 46:1, 55:22; 145:18-20; 147:3; Isaiah 40:29-31; Matthew 7:7-8; Philippians 4:7, 19; James 1:5. Write down each verse and the promise that is mentioned in that verse. Put this list in a place where you will be able to refer to it when you want to remember God's promises to you. As you learn of other promises, add them to the list.

2. Not all those who profess to be Christians are true believers. That is evident by what Jesus says in Matthew 8:12: "But the sons of the kingdom shall be cast out into outer darkness; there shall be weeping and gnashing of teeth." There are people who are superficially attached to Jesus yet don't submit to His lordship. Read Matthew 7:15-23. How can you know if a person is not a Christian? Can a corrupt person manifest good fruit? What does Jesus say will happen to the trees that do not bear good fruit? Verses 21-23 indicate that there will be people who appear to be doing miraculous works for the Lord, but never were of the Lord. According to Verse 23, why does Jesus tell them to depart from Him? What kind of fruit had they produced in their lives? Knowing this, how can we evaluate a person if we're doubtful that he's a Christian?

Matthew 13:3a, 10-17, 34, 35   Tape GC 2298

2
Kingdom Parables—Part 2

Outline

Introduction
A. The Insight
  1. Of the New Testament
  2. Of the Old Testament
     a) Zechariah 12:10-11a
     b) Zechariah 13:1
     c) Zechariah 14:4, 9
B. The Inquiry

Review
I. The place

Lesson
II. The Plan
  A. A Definition
  B. A Discussion
    1. Parables are instructive
    2. Parables are effective
  C. A Description
    1. The sower and the seed
    2. The wheat and the tares
    3. The mustard seed
    4. The leaven
    5. The treasure
    6. The merchant and the pearl
    7. The dragnet
III. The Purpose
  A. The Interpretation of a Word
    1. Explained
    2. Exemplified
  B. The Interpretation of the Parables
    1. Concealed
       a) The exception
       b) The exclusion
          (1) Explained
          (2) Expressed

16

    (*a*) By Jesus' parables
    (*b*) By Isaiah's prophecy
     i) The first fulfillment
     ii) The second fulfillment
  2. Revealed
   a) The present illumination
   b) The past inquisitiveness
IV. The Promise

 Conclusion

Introduction

In the chapters preceding Matthew 13, Matthew presents Jesus Christ as King. He shows us beyond a shadow of a doubt that Jesus is the anointed One of God, the Messiah, the Christ, the King, and the Savior of the world. John the Baptist said He would bring a kingdom. Jesus did what John the Baptist said He would—He offered a kingdom. He taught about the kingdom and called people to acknowledge Him as the King. However, the people rejected the King and refused His kingdom. That became a monumental point in redemptive history. The people of God—those called out of the loins of Abraham—were to be the channel through whom the world would be blessed. It was through them that the kingdom and the King would come (Gen. 12:2-3; Isa. 11:1-6). But they refused the King. Consequently, they had refused His kingdom, and, as we find out in Matthew 13, the kingdom was postponed. The kingdom couldn't come when the people of the King refused the King. So it was postponed to a future time when the people of Israel will accept the King and acknowledge His kingdom, and thereby receive it in its fullness.

 A. The Insight
  1. Of the New Testament

   The period of time between the rejection of Christ and His return is called "a mystery form of the kingdom." It is a time hidden from generations past—Jesus refers to the things of this time as "the mysteries" in Matthew 13:11. This period had never been described in all of revelatory history. It wasn't until Jesus describes this time in Matthew 13 that anyone knew the details of it. The rest of the New Testament builds on that description, but Matthew 13 is where it all began.

  2. Of the Old Testament

   For an idea of how the Old Testament saw this mystery period, look at the book of Zechariah. Chapters 12, 13, and 14 of Zechariah talk about the conversion of Israel and the establishment of the great kingdom of the Lord. Let's look at some of the specific details regarding that.

a) Zechariah 12:10-11*a*

"And I will pour upon the house of David, and upon the inhabitants of Jerusalem, the Spirit of grace and of supplications; and they shall look upon me whom they have pierced, and they shall mourn for him, as one mourneth for his only son, and shall be in bitterness for him, as one that is in bitterness for his firstborn. In that day shall there be a great mourning."

There is coming a day when the people of Israel will look upon the One they pierced (that speaks of the crucifixion) and will mourn that they ever harmed Him. That passage tells us that when the King came, He would be rejected and pierced. Both Psalm 22 and Isaiah 53 say the same thing. But later on, people will mourn that the King was rejected and crucified. However, Zechariah, the psalmist, and Isaiah say nothing about the time between Christ's rejection and return.

b) Zechariah 13:1

"In that day there shall be a fountain opened to the house of David and to the inhabitants of Jerusalem for sin and for uncleanness."

In other words, when they're sorry for their sin of rejecting the King and His kingdom, then God will pour out the fountain of salvation upon them.

c) Zechariah 14:4, 9

"And his feet shall stand in that day upon the Mount of Olives, which is before Jerusalem on the east, and the Mount of Olives shall cleave in its midst toward the east and toward the west, and there shall be a very great valley; and half of the mountain shall remove toward the north, and half of it toward the south [that describes the coming of the Lord]. . . . And the Lord shall be king over all the earth; in that day shall there be one Lord, and his name one."

The prophet Zechariah said there would be a rejection and a piercing, and later on, a mourning. Then he said there would be salvation for the people of God, and the establishment of the kingdom. But the period of time between the refusal of the King and the receiving of the King was never mentioned. That is the mystery period, hidden from generations past and never discussed in the pages of Holy Writ, until Jesus opens our understanding here in the thirteenth chapter of Matthew.

B. The Inquiry

The location of Matthew 13 is important. Anyone reading the gospel of Matthew, seeing Jesus come as the King, and seeing

Him and His kingdom refused, is immediately going to ask, "What happens now? If the kingdom is postponed until a future time, what will happen in the meantime?" That is precisely the question answered by the series of parables in Matthew 13. Each parable describes a particular facet of the period of time we now live in, otherwise known as the mystery form of the kingdom. It is also known as the church age. It will end when Jesus calls the church to be with Him.

Review

I. THE PLACE (vv. 1-2; see pp. 12-13)

Lesson

II. THE PLAN (vv. 3a, 34)

Verse 3 begins, "And he spoke many things unto them in parables." The plan of our Lord was to speak in parables. He had a very important reason for that, which we will see later. The phrase "he spoke many things unto them in parables" indicates to us that all of the parables in this chapter were spoken at one time. They were all spoken to the multitude on the seashore while Jesus sat and taught from a boat in the water (vv. 1-2). It is possible that the parables that appear in the other gospels were also given on that day and that Matthew didn't include them all. Jesus may have taught things that aren't even recorded in the Bible. Nonetheless, we know at that time, Jesus spoke many things to the crowd, all in parables. Verse 34 says, "All these things spoke Jesus unto the multitude in parables, and without a parable spoke he not unto them." He spoke only in parables, and He did not explain the parables to the multitude.

A. A Definition

What is a parable? The Greek word for *parable* is *parabolē*. *Para* means "something alongside of something else" so that a comparison can be made. It basically means "a comparison, or an illustration." If you have a spiritual truth that is hard to understand and lay alongside it a physical, earthly story that is easily understood, then you give understanding to that spiritual truth. That comparison is a parable.

The word *parabolē* is used in the Greek Old Testament (the Septuagint) forty-five times. That indicates that it was a very common form of Jewish teaching. It meant taking something very external, observable, objective, and earthly and laying it alongside something spiritual, supernatural, subjective, and heavenly so that people could understand the spiritual truth. It's an earthly story with a heavenly meaning.

B. A Discussion
   1. Parables are instructive

      A good teacher knows that you must communicate to people in terms of parables or analogies related to life. You can't just talk in abstraction. Difficult theological and spiritual concepts that are hard to understand need to be compared to things that are concrete and earthly so that people can understand the more difficult principles from those that are readily understood. In Matthew 13, Jesus teaches profound spiritual lessons about a period of time no one knew about, and He does it using simple terminology so that those who are supposed to understand Him will understand Him easily. In one parable, Jesus speaks of a field and grain, using birds, a road, thorns, and the sun in His story. In the rest of the chapter He refers to wheat and tares, a mustard seed, leaven, treasure, pearls, a fishing net, and a householder. Those were all things that were understood by the people of the agrarian culture in which Jesus taught.

   2. Parables are effective

      There are four reasons parables are effective. First, because they make truth concrete. In other words, because most people think in pictures, it is effective to take abstract concepts and make pictures out of them. We may not understand the concept of spreading the gospel, but we do understand it when it's pictured by a man throwing seed in a field. Parables help make truth concrete. Second, they make truth portable. By that I mean if you remember the story, you can always recover its spiritual meaning, because all of the elements are there in the story. A parable allows truth to be carried around in people's minds. Third, they make truth interesting. Parables can reduce rather dull thoughts into life situations that grab people's attention. Fourth, they make truth personally discoverable. In other words, as the story is told, you begin to internalize the spiritual truth that is being conveyed.

      So parables are a marvelous mode of teaching, because they make truth concrete, portable, interesting, and personally discoverable. Our Lord spoke in parables just as the Hebrews commonly spoke in parables (they used the term *mashal* to refer to parabolic teaching). It was His plan to use parables here.

C. A Description

   Let me just briefly introduce you to the parables and describe each one without reading the details. I want to draw out the truth that Jesus is teaching in each parable. As we read them, you will see the description of the church age. This is the first time it is ever described from the viewpoint of our Lord Jesus Christ.

1. The sower and the seed

    This parable starts from the last part of verse 3 and continues on to verse 23. Here, Jesus tells of a sower who went into the fields and sowed seeds. This depicts the preaching of the gospel throughout the world. The stony ground in this parable represents the people who will reject the gospel. Then there are some people who will initially receive the gospel, but thorns or the sun will cause them to fall away. Last, some people will initially receive the gospel and ultimately bring forth fruit. Jesus is saying this: The gospel will be preached throughout the world. Some will hear it and reject it; some will hear it and accept it for a while, but then fall away; yet some will hear it and believe and bring forth fruit. The principle here is very simple. We will never win the whole world to Christ.

    The second parable, in verses 24–30, is the parable of:

2. The wheat and the tares

    Jesus talks here of a man who sowed wheat in his field. While the man was asleep, an enemy came and sowed tares in the field. Tares look exactly like wheat and crowd the wheat and ruin the crop. But you can't pull them out because you can't tell the difference between the two until they're ready to harvest. The Lord is saying that there will be true believers and false believers during the church age. There will be people who say they belong to the kingdom, but in reality don't, and they will be alongside those who are genuine believers. Ultimately, God will put the wheat (true believers) in the barn and burn the tares (the false believers). The principle here is that we will never fully purge the church. The true and the false will coexist in the church until judgment.

3. The mustard seed

    This parable is in verses 31–32. It's about a mustard seed, which is one of the smallest of all seeds. This seed, when planted in the ground, grew and became a huge tree. The tree was so large that birds lived in it—it had large branches. Normally a mustard seed just produces a small bush. This parable is saying that the kingdom will begin small, and it will become worldwide. It will become widespread and influential and will be a haven for many people.

    The fourth parable, in verse 33, is the parable of:

4. The leaven

    Here Jesus likens the kingdom of heaven to leaven. The leaven represents the kingdom buried in the dough of the world. It will ultimately penetrate and permeate the whole earth. This parable shows the internal, permeating influence of the kingdom, which touches every dimension of human life.

5. The treasure

   This parable, in verse 44, talks about a treasure hidden in a field. A man was in this field (probably working in it), and he stumbled across the treasure. Rather than steal the treasure, he is honest and buys the whole field to get the treasure that's in it. Here the treasure represents salvation. When the man found it, he sold everything he owned to get it. The principle is that there will be people in this kingdom period who will give up everything they have to get salvation. The interesting thing about this parable is that the man wasn't looking for the treasure; He found it in the routine of his work day. It was while he was working that he was surprised by the reality of redemption. That tells us there will be many people who will come to know Jesus Christ by "stumbling" upon the grace of God.

   The next parable, in verses 45-46, is the parable of:

6. The merchant and the pearl

   Jesus describes here a man with the desire to find fine pearls. In his search, he finds a pearl that he wants very badly and sells everything he owns to purchase it.

   Just like the man in the last parable, this man is willing to pay the supreme price, which always involves giving up everything. They both gave up everything to purchase redemption. The difference is that this man was searching for the pearl, and that tells us there will be people in the kingdom who spend a great amount of time seeking the truth before they finally find it. Some people will come without ever seeking. They will be "surprised by joy," as C. S. Lewis put it. Other people will spend a lot of time and effort endeavoring to find the truth.

   The last parable, in verses 47-50, is about:

7. The dragnet

   Here a net was thrown into the sea, and many things were caught in it. After the net was pulled in, the good things were separated from the bad. This pictures the end of the church age, when Jesus brings everyone together and sorts out the true believers from the false.

   All those parables give tremendously profound insight into our time. We know each parable to be true of this time. The mystery kingdom is big. We have influenced the world and preached our message across the globe. The church has both good and evil—the wheat and the tares. We also know that as we proclaim the gospel, some reject it, some accept it for a little while, and some truly accept it and produce fruit. We know that the enemy attacks us. We know that we'll never be able to purge the church. And we know that there are people who search diligently for God, while others seem to stumble across God. Those are the characteristics of our time, and that is how it will be before the King returns.

So the Lord's plan is to teach in parables. Now, while parables can help make things clear, an unexplained parable is nothing but a riddle that is impossible to understand. That is why Jesus had to explain what they meant, even to His own disciples. Mark 4:10–11 records the same occasion as appears in Matthew 13 and says, "When he was alone, they that were about him with the twelve asked of him the parable. And he said unto them, Unto you it is given to know the mystery of the kingdom of God; but unto those who are outside, all these things are done in parables." Jesus only explained the parables to the twelve and to those who believed. Everyone else heard nothing but the unexplained parables.

III. THE PURPOSE (vv. 10–17)

In verses 10–11 we read, "The disciples came, and said unto him, Why speakest thou unto them in parables? He answered and said unto them, Because it is given unto you to know the mysteries of the kingdom of heaven, but to them it is not given." That tells us about the purpose of the parables. They were to reveal the truth to some and conceal it from others.

A. The Interpretation of a Word

1. Explained

Jesus said to His disciples, "It is given unto you to know the mysteries" (v. 11). When He said the word "mysteries," the cultural background of the disciples helped them to understand what He was saying. When we think of the word *mystery*, we think of Agatha Christie or some kind of whodunit. But in the Hellenistic world, mysteries were sacred secrets known only to the upper-level people in a religion. They were truths only for the initiated.

We have secret societies today, too, such as Freemasonry. In such groups only those who reach a certain level are told the secrets of the group. That's a heritage borne out of gnosticism (the word *gnostic* comes from the Greek word *gnōsis*, which means "to know"). The mystery religions of Greece, which were borne out of Babylon, contained secrets that you learned as you moved up in rank.

2. Exemplified

One of the most famous mysteries was that of Isis and Osiris. Osiris was a wise and good king in Egypt. Seth, his wicked brother, hated him. He, with seventy-two conspirators, persuaded Osiris to come to a banquet. When he came to the banquet, Seth put him in a coffin and threw him in the Nile River. Isis, the wife of Osiris, found the coffin and brought it home. Seth came again and cut Osiris's body into fourteen pieces and shipped them to fourteen locations throughout Egypt. But Isis found all the pieces, and somehow Osiris rose from the dead. Now, only the initiated people were told what that story meant. Every part of that story had a secret. It talked about good versus evil, the sorrowing search of love, the triumphal discovery when love finds its object, and the conquering of death. The ultimate secret was that if you, as a worshiper, said to Osiris, "I am thou and thou art I," you would then be placed in union with Osiris and live forever. Without the explanation, you could only do your best to try to make sense out of the story.

B. The Interpretation of the Parables

Jesus said to the disciples, "The secrets about the kingdom of heaven—the mysteries—I will give to you to know. But for those who reject Me, I will not explain the mysteries." So the Lord both reveals and conceals the truths about the kingdom of heaven. Let's look now at the interpretation of the parables.

1. Concealed (vv. 12–15)

   a) The exception (v. 12*a*)

   "For whosoever hath, to him shall be given, and he shall have more abundance."

   The phrase "for whosoever hath" refers to those who have received from God all that comes to believers. Jesus is saying that whoever is regenerate—whoever has received the King and therefore identifies with Him—and has accepted God's truth, will get more of God's truth. That speaks of enlightenment. The person who has God's truth will get more of it. A parable that illustrates that principle is in Matthew 25:14–30. An unfaithful servant who was entrusted with a little of his master's money had it taken away from him, and it was given to a servant who had been faithful with larger amounts of that master's money (v. 28).

   God will give an ascending revelation of truth to the person who accepts the King and His kingdom. To those who live up to the light of Christ, He will give more light.

   b) The exclusion (vv. 12*b*–15)

   (1) Explained (v. 12*b*)

   "But whosoever hath not, from him shall be taken away even what he hath."

The King had come. He had taught, He had preached, and He had done miracle after miracle. The Jewish people had some understanding of who He was and had been given a foretaste of the kingdom. They had seen the signs and wonders of the Spirit of God. However, when they rejected the King, they lost even what they had previously understood. None of what they saw made sense anymore, and they began to descend into deeper darkness.

That disorientation is still evident today. No other group in our society has lost the original meaning of their religion in quite the way the Jewish people have. Paul says in Romans 9 that they had the covenants, the promises, and the gifts of God. They were adopted by God and had the patriarchs (vv. 4-5). Yet as soon as they rejected the King, God turned the lights out on them, and they began to lose the understanding of everything they had. The religion the Jewish people ascribed to no longer made sense to them. That's why some of Judaism has moved from an Orthodox position to a Conservative position and then to a Reformed position, which teaches that the Bible is not the Word of God. The descent into darkness has continued since the time they rejected Christ.

If you accept the light that Christ gives, then more light will be given. If you refuse that light, then deeper darkness will ensue. The parable of the servants and the talents shows that (Matt. 25:14-30). Jesus said that those who reject Him will lose what they have, and it will be given to those who respond to Him. That shows us that all men are progressing one way or the other; they never stay the same. The longer a man knows Jesus Christ, the more truth he receives. The longer a man refuses Jesus Christ, the deeper the pit of darkness becomes.

(2) Expressed (vv. 13-15)

   (*a*) By Jesus' parables (v. 13)

      "Therefore speak I to them in parables, because they seeing, see not; and hearing, they hear not, neither do they understand."

      Jesus is saying, "I speak to them in parables because this is an act of judgment. Because they will not see and hear while they can understand, I will now speak to them so they cannot understand." The willful rejection of Christ by man has brought the judicial rejection of Christ. Man says no to God, so God says no to man. By doing that, God is simply confirming the stubbornness of man. For those who rejected Christ, the parables became interesting stories they couldn't understand.

(b) By Isaiah's prophecy (vv. 14-15)

"And in them is fulfilled the prophecy of Isaiah, which saith, By hearing, ye shall hear and shall not understand; and seeing, ye shall see and shall not perceive; for this people's heart is become gross, and their ears are dull of hearing, and their eyes they have closed, lest at any time they should see with their eyes, and hear with their ears, and should understand with their heart, and should be converted, and I should heal them."

i) The first fulfillment

This prophecy appears in Isaiah 6:9-10. Isaiah had pronounced overwhelming judgment on Israel. He had already cursed the people for their drunkenness, debauchery, immorality, bribery, oppression of the poor, and hypocritical religion. At the height of Isaiah's pronouncements, King Uzziah died, and the country plunged into the darkest days of its history. The Babylonian captivity was their imminent judgment. Then Isaiah says in 6:9-10, "God is going to judge you. You wouldn't hear and see Him, so now you can't hear and see. You wouldn't be converted and healed, so now you can't be converted and healed." Jeremiah echoed the message of Isaiah, and not long after came the Babylonian captivity. That was the first fulfillment of Isaiah's prophecy, and Matthew 13:14-15 says that the rejection of Jesus was the second fulfillment of that prophecy.

ii) The second fulfillment

The parables, then, are an expression of judgment on those who refused to believe. The fact that man does not understand the things of God doesn't just testify to his ignorance, it also testifies to God's judgment. Believers understand the Bible not because of their intellect, but because God graciously illuminates their hearts and minds.

There were three steps in this second fulfillment.

Step 1

When Jesus first came, His words were very clear. He said that He was the King and proved His claim. He preached the kingdom message, "Repent; for the kingdom of heaven is at hand" (Matt. 4:17).

Step 2

But the people didn't listen to Him and rejected Him. In Matthew 5-7 Jesus uses clear analogies that refer to salt, light, birds, and the lilies of the field and sums up everything by saying, "Seek ye first the kingdom . . . and all these things shall be added unto you" (6:33); yet people hardened their hearts. They blasphemed Him by saying He was from Satan. So now He spoke to them in riddles that He wouldn't explain.

Step 3

In 1 Corinthians 14:21 we find another of Isaiah's pronouncements of judgment upon Israel. The verse quotes Isaiah 28:11-12 and says, "It is written, with men of other tongues and other lips will I speak unto this people; and yet for all that will they not hear me, saith the Lord." Verse 22 continues, "Wherefore, tongues are for a sign, not to them that believe, but to them that believe not."

People always ask me, "What are tongues for?" It says in 1 Corinthians 14:22 that they are a sign, not for those who believe, but for those who don't believe. The primary use of tongues occurred on the Day of Pentecost in front of the unbelieving Israelites. The people wouldn't listen to Christ when He spoke clearly to them, so He judged them by speaking in riddles. After that, He judged them by speaking to them in a language they didn't even know. Tongues are a sign of God's judgment upon Israel.

So Jesus said that the prophecy of Isaiah was being fulfilled by those who rejected Him. Incidentally, that prophecy is quoted no less than five times in the New Testament. Each time it is quoted, it is in relation to Israel's rejection of Christ.

Jesus not only concealed the truths about the kingdom of heaven, but He also made them:

2. Revealed (vv. 16–17)

   a) The present illumination (v. 16)

   "But blessed are your eyes, for they see; and your ears, for they hear."

   Isn't that wonderful? We understand the parables because Jesus explained them. We also have the New Testament text to read from and the Spirit of God as our Teacher.

   Mark 4:34, a parallel verse on this same incident, says, "He expounded all things to his disciples." In Matthew 13:51, Jesus says to the disciples, "Have ye understood all these things? They say unto him, Yea, Lord." They didn't understand those things because they were smart; they understood because they possessed the illuminating presence of Jesus Christ.

   Luke 24:45 says, "Then opened he their [the disciples'] understanding, that they might understand the scriptures." Did you know that even if a person is saved, he will not understand the Scripture without the illuminating work of the Spirit of God? That is why in Psalm 119:18 the psalmist cries out, "Open thou mine eyes, that I may behold wondrous things out of thy law." Isaiah means the same thing in Isaiah 64:1 when he says, "Oh, that thou wouldest rend the heavens, that thou wouldest come down." Let me clarify what he meant by that.

   b) The past inquisitiveness (v. 17)

   "For verily I say unto you that many prophets and righteous men have desired to see those things which ye see, and have not seen them; and to hear those things which ye hear, and have not heard them."

   Isaiah wasn't alive when the heavens were rent and when Jesus came down. Hebrews 11:40 says that the salvation of the Old Testament saints did not become complete until our time (the time of Christianity). Peter said that the Old Testament prophets had looked into their own prophecies, hoping to find out what person and what time would fulfill the prophecies (1 Pet. 1:10–11). They didn't get to see what others saw. The disciples saw the heavens rent and God come down in human flesh to reveal His truth, and we have the resident Holy Spirit to lead us into all truth. 1 Corinthians 2:10 says that the Holy Spirit searches the deep things of God and reveals them to us. We understand the truths of God because we have divine illumination. That doesn't mean we don't need to study the Bible—we should study to keep from being ashamed (2 Tim. 2:15). When we discipline ourselves to study, we open ourselves to the illumination of the Spirit of God.

So Jesus' parables conceal God's truth as an act of judgment against Israel. At the same time, they reveal God's truth, because Jesus explained the parables to those who believed. Although Jesus is not here today to explain the Word to us, when He left earth He promised that the Holy Spirit would lead us into all truth (John 16:13).

Do you realize what a privilege we have? We not only have the Bible, but we have its Author living in us, explaining it to us! The saints of old really hungered for that!

We've seen the place, the plan, and the purpose. Let's look now at:

IV. THE PROMISE (v. 35)

There is one question that many people ask: If the King offered the kingdom and it was rejected, then doesn't that foul up God's plan? In other words, because the kingdom wasn't accepted, does God have to alter His plans? Was the mystery age something that God had to add to His plans when things didn't go the way they were supposed to?

Verse 35 says that Jesus spoke in parables "that it might be fulfilled which was spoken by the prophet, saying, I will open my mouth in parables; I will utter things which have been kept secret from the foundation of the world." That was quoted from Psalm 78:2, a psalm written by Asaph the prophet (2 Chron. 29:30). Asaph predicted that the Messiah would one day speak in parables as an act of judgment and that He would reveal to believers a secret kept from the foundation of the world. Therefore we know that God didn't have to alter His plans. He knew that Israel would reject the King and that there would be a mystery age. What does that tell us? It tells us that God's plan is on schedule. He is sovereign, and He is not making alterations to His schedule as time goes along.

Conclusion

There are some profound lessons to be learned from what we've just studied. Let's sum them up. First, truth is only available to people who believe and are taught by God. Second, those who reject Jesus Christ only descend deeper into the darkness of their unbelief. And third, God's plan is right on schedule. It's big enough to encompass the unbelief of Israel and the mystery of this age.

Focusing on the Facts

1. Will the people of Israel always reject Christ? Why or why not? Use Scripture to support your answer (see pp. 17-18).
2. Explain what the word *parable* means, and explain what a parable does (see pp. 19-20).

3. Why is it important to use parables or analogies (see p. 20)?
4. Give four reasons parables are effective teaching instruments. Explain each of the reasons (see p. 20).
5. What does the stony ground represent in the parable of the sower and the seed? What other responses will people have to the gospel? What is the principle of the parable (see p. 21)?
6. In the parable of the wheat and the tares, why are tares so troublesome? What principle is being taught here (see p. 21)?
7. What is unusual about the plant produced by the mustard seed in the parable of the mustard seed? What is that parable teaching about the church age (see p. 21)?
8. In the parable of the leaven, what is the leaven likened to? What does that parable illustrate (see p. 21)?
9. What does the treasure represent in the parable of the treasure? How did the man go about obtaining the treasure? What does the fact that the man accidentally stumbled across the treasure indicate (see p. 22)?
10. In the parable of the merchant and the pearl, how did the merchant go about obtaining the pearl? What difference is there between this parable and the parable of the treasure (see p. 22)?
11. Into what two categories was the catch divided in the parable of the dragnet? What do they represent (see pp. 22-23)?
12. Whom did Jesus explain the parables to? Whom did Jesus not explain the parables to (see p. 23)?
13. What was Jesus' purpose in speaking in parables (see p. 23)?
14. What was the definition of a mystery, according to the Hellenistic world (see p. 23)?
15. What does the phrase "for whosoever hath" in Matthew 13:12*a* mean? What parable in Matthew illustrates the principle behind that? Describe what happens in that parable (see pp. 24-25).
16. What happened to the understanding the Jewish people had of Christ when they rejected Him? What has happened to the Jewish people and Judaism over the years to show that (see p. 25)?
17. Matthew 13:14-15 quotes Isaiah 6:9-10. Before Isaiah pronounced judgment, what had he condemned the people for? How was God's judgment made manifest to Israel (see p. 26)?
18. The parables are an expression of _____ on those who refused to believe (see p. 26).
19. The fact that man does not understand the things of God doesn't just testify to his ignorance, it also testifies to _____. Why is it that believers are able to understand the Bible (see p. 26)?
20. What are tongues a sign of (1 Cor. 14:22; see p. 27)?

21. Using Scripture, support the fact that Jesus helped the disciples to understand what He said (see p. 28).
22. What was the desire of many Old Testament prophets and righteous men, according to Matthew 13:17? According to 1 Peter 1:10-11, what were the Old Testament prophets searching for (see p. 28)?
23. Did God have to change His plans for everything when Israel rejected Christ? How does Matthew 13:35 indicate that God knew Israel would reject Christ (see p. 29)?

Pondering the Principles

1. In Matthew 13 we see that Jesus taught the multitude by the seashore using parables. His purpose was to speak in unexplained riddles to those who rejected Him and to reveal truths about the mystery form of the kingdom to those who believed Him. What kind of terminology did Jesus use in the parables (see p. 20)? Why would it be important for us to understand the cultural background that the parables were told in? Would you have understood the significance of the mustard tree in Matthew 13:31-32 without knowing that mustard seeds normally produce a small bush? Does the overview of the seven parables in Matthew 13 begin to reveal to you the thorough way that Jesus taught? Why, then, should we be thorough in Bible study? Make it a habit not only to read God's Word, but to study it with the desire to understand what God is teaching in the Scripture.

2. In the parables of the treasure and the pearl, the men who found objects of worth recognized their true value upon seeing them. That is evidenced by the fact that they were willing to give up everything they owned to purchase what they knew was of greater value. Is that true in your life with regard to your relationship with God? How much do you value your relationship with God in comparison to how you value other things? Ask God to help you have your heart's desire in the right place.

3. When did Jesus begin to speak in parables? Before or after the people rejected him? Read the account in Nehemiah 9:6-37. What wonderful things did the Lord do for the Israelites in verses 9-15? How did the Israelites respond in verses 16-17a, 18? What was God's response in verses 17b, 19-21? After God graciously gave the Israelites the Promised Land, what happened (v. 26)? What attribute of God was continually shown to the Israelites in verses 27-31, despite their rebellion? Verse 33 sums up the whole situation: "Howbeit, thou art just in all that is brought upon us; for thou hast done right, but we have done wickedly." What does that passage teach us about God's judgments upon men? Do you think God is fair to men when He judges them? Pray right now to God and thank Him for His patience and mercy to you despite your sinfulness.

Matthew 13:3b-9, 18-23 Tape GC 2299

3
The Responses to the Gospel

Outline

Introduction

Lesson
I. The Instruction of the Parable
   A. The Explanation
      1. The sower
      2. The soils
         a) The wayside soil
         b) The stony soil
         c) The weedy soil
         d) The good soil
   B. The Exhortation
II. The Interpretation of the Parable
   A. The Sower
   B. The Seed
   C. The Soils
      1. The receptiveness of the soils
      2. The responses of the soils
         a) The wayside hearer
            (1) Beheld
            (2) Blinded
         b) The stony hearer
            (1) The immediate thrill
            (2) The imminent trouble
               (a) The adversity
                  i) Explained
                  ii) Expected
               (b) The apostasy
         c) The weedy hearer
            (1) The preoccupation depicted
            (2) The purification demanded
         d) The fruitful hearer
            (1) The promise
            (2) The product
               (a) Manifest
               (b) Multiplied

Conclusion
A. The Requirement for Self-Examination
B. The Requirement for Self-Confidence

Introduction

In this lesson we begin an in-depth look at the parables of Matthew 13. We have learned that the parables were given by our Lord to describe the character of the kingdom between His rejection and His return. Those parables describe the church age—the mystery form of the kingdom. Christ is the King, and His kingdom is here now, but it's a form of the kingdom that was not seen in the Old Testament. There is coming a day when He will return to establish His prophesied earthly kingdom, but in the meantime, the mystery form of the kingdom is here. We asked the question, "What will this period of time be like?" Our Lord answered that question for His disciples here in a series of seven parables. They clearly explain to us the very time in which we live.

We also learned that the Lord knew how to take the natural world and wield it as a weapon of great precision in giving instruction about spiritual truth. He was able to take something that people could understand and lay it alongside something they did not understand so they could grasp the more difficult concept. That's what a parable is. It's a comparison. Each of the parables here is filled with profound spiritual truth. I have found that the longer you study them, the more rich and full they become. The amazing thing is that with all of the richness and wide-ranging ramifications of each parable, our Lord is able to tell each one in a simple, concise manner. He had the supernatural capability of using a bare minimum of terms and yet expressing incredible profundity.

Lesson

I. THE INSTRUCTION OF THE PARABLE (vv. 3*b*–9)

A. The Explanation (vv. 3*b*–8)

1. The sower (v. 3*b*)

"Behold, a sower went forth to sow."

Because of the agricultural way of life in that part of the world, everybody understood the process of sowing seeds. Jesus spoke of something that everyone was familiar with. It may have been that as Jesus was teaching the multitude, there was in the distance a sower in his field.

When sowing seed, a sower would drape a bag over his shoulder that had an opening at the top. After the furrows had been prepared, the sower would take the seed from the bag and broadcast it. That was the original meaning of the English word *broadcast*. He would scatter the seed into the furrow as he walked along the furrow in a straight line with orderly steps. When he reached the end of one furrow, he would turn and start up the next furrow, never missing a step and still throwing the seed. That is how a field was sowed.

Jesus indicates that as the sower throws the seed, there are four kinds of soil that seed will fall on. Let's look at them:

2. The soils (vv. 4–8)

   a) The wayside soil (v. 4)

   "And when he sowed, some of the seeds fell by the wayside, and the fowls came and devoured them."

   Palestine, in those days, was literally crisscrossed with fields. The fields were usually long narrow strips separated from other fields by paths. The paths between the fields were narrow—about three feet wide. They were used by the farmer to get to whatever field he wanted to reach. They were also used by the travelers who were going from one part of the country to another. In Matthew 12:1, we see the Lord Jesus Christ and His disciples walking through the fields of grain, and no doubt they were walking on those little paths. There were no fences or walls around the fields, just those narrow paths for travelers and for the farmer to get around in his area.

   It was those paths that the Lord had in mind when He talked about the wayside. The dirt in those paths was packed down, uncultivated, and never loosened. The continual pounding of the dirt by men's feet and the dryness of that part of the world would compact the dirt to the point that it was like a road. It became as hard as pavement. As a result, if a farmer threw the seed and some of it went beyond the furrow only to land on that hard surface, it would never grow. It could not penetrate the ground. As the farmer was sowing the seed, there would be birds hovering above him, waiting for the opportunity to eat any seed that landed on the hard path. Whatever seed the birds did not eat would be trampled by the feet of men that were passing through the fields (Luke 8:5).

   b) The stony soil (vv. 5–6)

   "Some [seed] fell upon stony places, where they had not much earth; and forthwith they sprang up, because they had no deepness of earth. And when the sun was up, they were scorched; and because they had no root, they withered away."

   Luke adds that the seed that landed upon the stony soil "lacked moisture" (8:6). There wasn't any root to capture the moisture. Now, Jesus is not talking about soil with rocks in it, because any farmer who cultivated a field would make sure all the rocks were out. But the land in Israel has strains of limestone bedrock running through it, and in many places this bedrock comes up to within inches of the soil surface. Farmers sometimes were unaware of the bedrock. Consequently, they left areas that weren't broken up in the cultivating process. If the seed landed on that hard rock, it would germinate and try to send its roots downward, but there was no place for the roots to go. Initially, those seeds would spring up higher than the other grain (because they could only grow up and didn't use their energy to send roots downward, like other seeds). But eventually they died from the heat of the summer, because the bedrock hindered their roots from finding any moisture.

c) The weedy soil (v. 7)

"And some fell among thorns; and the thorns sprang up, and choked them."

Initially, the weedy soil looks good. It's deep, it's rich, and it's cultivated. It looks ready for planting. But after the seeds are sown and they begin to germinate, weeds also begin to grow from the fibrous weed roots hidden in the ground. The weeds then choke the life out of the grain. Weeds are natural to that soil; they're at home there. Grain seeds are a foreign element in that soil. Because of that, the grain has to be cultivated. The weeds eventually choke the grain and send out their leaves so that they take up the sun and the moisture. There's not enough room for both to share the nutrients of that soil. Thus, the good seed dies.

d) The good soil (v. 8)

"But other seeds fell into good ground, and brought forth fruit, some an hundredfold, some sixtyfold, some thirtyfold."

The soil here is soft, deep, and clean. It's soft, unlike the hard wayside soil. It's deep, unlike the stony limestone ground. And it's clean, unlike the weed-infested soil. It's on this ground that the seeds burst to life and bring forth a tremendous harvest, sometimes a hundredfold, or sixtyfold, or thirtyfold. By the way, the average yield would be 7.5–fold. A good crop would be tenfold. So Jesus is talking about a tremendous, flourishing crop.

The parable is very simple. A man goes out and throws seed. The seed falls onto four kinds of soils. Some fall on a hard path where they will never germinate. They're either picked up by birds or trampled under the feet of those who walk on the path. Some seeds fall onto rocky soil and begin to grow. But the growth is all upward and the roots are very shallow, so the sun eventually scorches the plant because the roots cannot find moisture in the rock. There are seeds that fall on the weedy ground and become strangled by the weeds that already live there and are natural to that place. Last, there are seeds that fall into good, clean, deep, rich, soft soil and product a tremendous harvest.

B. The Exhortation (v. 9)

"Who hath ears to hear, let him hear."

What does Jesus mean by that? He is saying, "If you understand this, then pay attention, because there is an important message here." You ask, "Who is the one that can hear?" Verses 10-17 explain that the only people who can understand parables are those who believe in the King—those who are redeemed. If you are in the kingdom, the King promises to explain to you the meaning of what He says. Becoming a Christian doesn't mean that you get instant wisdom so you can understand everything on your own. It means that God promises to teach you the meaning of His Word.

The people who can't understand Jesus are those with the hard hearts and the deaf ears. In Matthew 13:14-15, Jesus quotes Isaiah 6:9-10, "For this people's heart is become gross, and their ears are dull of hearing, and their eyes they have closed" (v. 15). The people who reject Jesus won't be able to understand what He is talking about. Only those who believe in Jesus will understand. "Blessed are your eyes, for they see; and your ears, for they hear" (v. 16). The parables conceal from those who don't believe, and reveal to those who do. In Mark 4:10-20, Jesus is asked by the disciples the meaning of the parable of the sower and the seed, and He explains it to them apart from the multitude.

So Jesus is saying, "You who are able to understand, hear what I say." Then starting in verse 18, He explains the spiritual message He is trying to convey.

II. THE INTERPRETATION OF THE PARABLE (vv. 18-23)

A. The Sower (v. 18)

"Hear, therefore, the parable of the sower."

Who is the sower? The sower in this parable is the Lord Jesus Christ. That is confirmed later on in the chapter as the Lord explains a different parable in which wheat was sown, and He tells His disciples. "He that soweth the good seed is the Son of man" (v. 37*b*). The Lord is the original sower. He is the One who first puts the seed in the soil.

You say, "What is the seed?" In verse 19 we read, "When any one heareth the word of the kingdom." The seed is the Word of

God, and the first sower of the gospel was the Lord Himself. Anyone who sows what Jesus first sowed is also a sower! Mark 4:14 says, "The sower soweth the word." Those of us who love Christ, receive His message, and pass it on are sowers of the Word. The seed is the Word of God, and we are sowing the message of the kingdom.

B. The Seed (v. 19*a*)

Verse 19 tells us that the seed is the Word of the kingdom. It is God's revelation. Luke 8:11, a parallel passage giving the same parable, says, "The seed is the word of God." The gospel is the message about the King and his kingdom.

I would like to add something worthy of note. Seeds cannot be created. If we didn't have seeds, we could never grow things. We are dependent on what grows and produces more seeds because God originally created seeds and seeds reproduce themselves. They are things that we'd never be able to reproduce. The same is true with the seed of the Word of God. The Lord does not call on us to create our own message. He says, "Take that which has already been sown and sow it again." We are not to produce a new supply of information; we are to build upon the revelation of the Word of God. We are utterly dependent, then, upon divine revelation—as much as we are dependent on God creating the seeds that reproduce themselves and bring us the fruit we eat today.

The parable, then, is about preaching the gospel—the Word about the King and His kingdom. It's about telling men that Jesus is the King, that He will bring an earthly kingdom and how to be in that kingdom. All of those things are involved in preaching.

C. The Soils (vv. 19-23)

1. The receptiveness of the soils

This is the main import of the parable: It shows how men will respond to the gospel. We've seen that there are four kinds of soils. All the soils are basically the same—the only difference is whether the dirt is hard, has rock underneath it, has weeds in it, or is good. The issue is not the soil, rather, it is the condition of the soil. That means that all men *could* receive the seed. All soil could receive the seed if it was broken up and cleaned of weeds. So the key to the parable is that person's response to the gospel depends upon the condition of that person's heart. We know that the soil refers to the heart because verse 19 says, "When any one heareth the word of the kingdom, and understandeth it not, then cometh the wicked one, and catcheth away that which was sown in his heart." The condition of the heart determines how receptive a person is to the gospel.

When the disciples saw that Jesus was being rejected, they probably asked Him, "Lord, what is going to happen now? You've been blasphemed and rejected, and the kingdom cannot come." Using the parable of the sower and the seed as an illustration, He says, "I'll tell you what's going to happen. You're going to go out just like I did and sow the seed, which is the Word of God. You're going to preach the same message about the same King and the same kingdom." Jesus talked about the different soils in the parable to encourage the apostles: "There will be the wayside soil, the stony soil, and the weedy soil, and you've got to know about that, or you could become disillusioned. But there will also be the good soil that will bring forth thirty, sixty, or a hundredfold." The parable was intended to help the apostles approach the ministry with excitement and anticipation that God was going to produce results.

Before we examine the four kinds of responses to the gospel, remember this: Salvation is manifested by fruit, not foliage. That is imporant to know, or the parable can become confusing. Keep in mind too that those four kinds of responses are characterisic of our day.

2. The responses of the soils

   a) The wayside hearer (v. 19)

   "When any one heareth the word of the kingdom, and understandeth it not, then cometh the wicked one, and catcheth away that which was sown in his heart. This is he which received seed by the wayside."

   In other words, the seed that fell on the wayside couldn't penetrate the ground, and birds hovered nearby waiting to snatch the seed when the farmer turned his back. Luke adds that any seeds the birds missed were trampled by men (Luke 8:5). That illustrates the man who is heardhearted. The Old Testament would call this man stiff-necked. He is unresponsive and indifferent. The gospel message just hits him and bounces off. Satan, represented by the birds, comes and snatches that seed away. That confirms what the Lord said earlier, "Whosoever hath not, from him shall be taken away even what he hath" (v. 12*b*). This man's heart has been so pounded down by the mixed multitude of sins in his life that there's no sensitivity at all. His heart knows no repentance—no sorrow for sin, no guilt, no concern over the things that really matter. He allows his heart to be trampled down by sin day after day; it is never broken up or softened by conviction.

   (1) Beheld

   The fool in the book of Proverbs illustrates that kind of man. He despises wisdom (Prov. 1:7), hates instruction (Prov. 15:5), is stiff-necked and hardhearted (Prov. 27:22), will not listen (Prov. 23:9), and says in his heart that there is no God (Ps. 14:1). He does not want to be bothered with the message of the gospel. He says, "Leave me alone!" I'm sure we've all met people like him. We throw the seed, which just bounces, and then Satan comes and snatches it away.

(2) Blinded

The wayside hearer is blinded by Satan, the god of this age, who "hath blinded the minds of them who believe not, lest the light of the glorious gospel of Christ, who is the image of God, should shine unto them" (2 Cor. 4:4). In other words, when someone does not respond to the gospel, Satan blinds that person to the true value of the gospel.

There are many ways that Satan blinds people. One way he does that is by sending false teachers to those who have heard the gospel. Those false teachers tell people not to believe what they've heard. Another way Satan snatches the seed is by making a man fearful. People don't respond to the gospel because they're afraid they'll lose their reputation, be rejected by their friends, or be considered a religious fanatic. Sometimes Satan uses pride. There are people who don't want to admit they need help or that there are some things they don't know. Satan will use doubt, prejudice, stubbornness, a person's love of sin, and procrastination to snatch away the gospel. He will use whatever way he can or whatever combination of ways necessary to make a person forget that he ever heard the gospel message.

I encourage you to examine yourself and see if you are one of the many people like that. Examine your heart and see if you are that dry, hard road on the edge of the field. You may be on the fringes of religion, but sins have just pounded down the dirt of your heart until it is utterly unproductive and unresponsive to God.

Jesus told us that we're to expect this. There will be people who are very close to the truth and yet remain shut to it. We're to expect that kind of response to the gospel.

b) The stony hearer (vv. 20–21)

(1) The immediate thrill (v. 20)

"But he that received the seed in stony places, the same is he that heareth the word, and immediately with joy receiveth it"

This is the person who hears the Word and immediately receives it with joy. There isn't a lot of thought involved. It's just a quick response, an emotional, instant excitement that doesn't count the cost of following Christ or understand the significance of the gospel. There's a good feeling within this person and a lot of joy; he really seems to be growing. But it's all external because there hasn't been any true repentance or brokenness over sin, as indicated by the bedrock of resistance still under the soft surface of the ground.

There are people like that today. They never deal with the real issues. They just jump on the Jesus bandwagon because it looks so good. Those people seem to be growing faster than everyone else. They appear to have real joy and real tears. But three months later, they are gone. They were just excited over all the euphoria. Perhaps they said they were Christians just to be able to get married to Christians. They may have been trying to deal with a deep problem and reached out to Christianity in an attempt to find an instant solution. They thought, "Now I've got God on my side!" They may have been the recipients of inadequate evangelism. Possibly they were told that everything would be wonderful, happy, and joyful if they just accepted Jesus. But the soil underneath was never really plowed with the conviction of sin. They're like the man who built his house on the sand (Matt. 7:26–27). The religious structure is there, but there's nothing but superficial joy holding it up.

Now, when you look at the field of growing grain, you notice that those people stick out because they're taller than everyone else. You're excited because their growth seems to be real. However, when you come back in the heat of the summer, when the moisture is very limited, those people are dead. Verse 21 explains why.

(2) The imminent trouble (v. 21)

    (*a*) The adversity (v. 21*a*)

        "Yet hath he not root in himself, but endureth for a while; for when tribulation or persecution [Gk., *thlipsis*] ariseth because of the word."

        i) Explained

            This person has never been redeemed. He's never really been a genuine believer. He endures for a while and then falls away when tribulation and persecution come along. He faces suffering because he appears to belong to Christ and experiences pressure from the expectation of living the Christian life. He feels overwhelmed by those who want to get him into a Bible study, prayer meeting, or a discipling relationship. He experiences persecution because people criticize him for becoming a Christian. Because there is no root in this person, he won't survive the persecution. The nonreality of his initial response to the gospel will become evident.

This information is very helpful because it tells us to expect that to happen. When I pray with someone to receive Jesus Christ, I know that he might be that kind of person. When you see someone give an immediate, euphoric response to the gospel, keep in mind that he might still be rocky soil. There may not have been a sense of brokenness and a counting of the costs of following Christ (Matt. 16:24).

William Arnot said in 1869, "If the law of God has never rent the 'stony heart' and made it contrite, that is, bruised it small, you may, by receiving the gospel on some temporary, superficial softness of nature, obtain your religion more easily and quickly than others who have been more deeply exercised; but you may not retain it. He that endureth to the end shall be saved, but he that fails in the middle shall not." (*The Parables of Our Lord* [London: Nelson, 1869]).

ii) Expected

Second Timothy 3:12 says that all who live godly in this present age "shall suffer persecution." We are to expect that there will be those who will leave when persecution and pressure comes. I've dealt with such people, baptizing them, praying with them, and discipling them, but I can't tell their superficiality until the persecution comes.

(*b*) The apostasy (v. 21*b*)

"He is offended."

This means that he is trapped or caught by the persecution and will fall away. So watch for the conversion that's all smiles and cheers and lacks remorse, conviction, and repentance, such as that described in the Beatitudes (Matt. 5:1–12). We are to watch for that superficial kind of response to the gospel in cases where the person professed to become a Christian as a result of a superficial presentation of the gospel given on television or by other means.

Trouble and persecution, then, are very important to the kingdom of God, for two reasons. First, trouble and persecution will make false believers fall away from the church. Second, trouble and persecution will strengthen true believers. First Peter 5:10 tells us that after we have suffered, the Lord will make us perfect. We should desire trouble and persecution because they discourage false believers and strengthen true believers.

If your confession of Christ does not come from a deep, inner conviction of your sin, does not include a tremendous desire for the Lord to purify and lead you, and does not involve self-sacrifice and a willingness to suffer for His sake, then you have no root. It will only be a matter of time before persecution comes along, and you'll fall away. You won't endure the persecution because you're not willing to take up the cross and follow Him (Matt. 16:24). If you don't take up the cross, you're not worthy to be His disciple. If you've got a stony heart, only God can break it. You'll need to pray and ask the Lord to do for you what He promised to do for Israel in Ezekiel 36:26: "I will take away the stony heart out of your flesh, and I will give you an heart of flesh."

c) The weedy hearer (v. 22)

"He also that received seed among the thorns is he that heareth the word; and the care of this age, and the deceitfulness of riches, choke the word, and he becometh unfruitful."

(1) The preoccupation depicted

The phrase "the care of this age" refers to worldliness, and the phrase, "the deceitfulness of riches" refers to the fact that the worlds riches are deceptive. In other words, it is the mundane things of the world—your career, house, car, wardrobe, prestige, looks, and riches—that are deceitful. First Timothy 6:9–10 says, "They that will be rich fall into a temptation and a snare . . . for the love of money is the root of all evil, which, while some coveted after, they have erred from the faith, and pierced themselves through with many sorrows."

(2) The purification demanded

Jesus is saying here that there will be those who listen but never clean out the soil. The things of the world are still in the person's heart. That's why Jesus said, "No man can serve two masters; for either he will hate the one, and love the other; or else he will hold to the one, and despise the other. Ye cannot serve God and money" (Matt. 6:24). John said, "If any man love the world, the love of the Father is not in him" (1 John 2:15b). You can't be a double-minded man. The soil that is going to produce fruit must be cleansed of worldliness. That's why true salvation only occurs when there's a willingness to deal with sin in one's life. True salvation is a marvelous and gracious work of God.

I know there are people who say, "You don't have to do anything to be saved. Just believe and that's it." The soil may look good, but it's impure. That is an example of someone trying to hold on to everything. He wants the Word of God and everything else at the same time. Now, worldliness is indigenous to the heart, just as weeds are indigenous to soil. When you introduce a seed that is foreign to that soil (just as you would introduce the gospel to the heart), it has to be cared for; otherwise, it won't survive. The ground has only so much nourishment. If the ground is busy nourishing all the weeds, it won't be able to help the seed survive.

There is nothing wrong with the sower, seed, or soil here. The condition of the soil is the problem. People who profess to be saved aren't saved if their hearts are still occupied with the things of the world. In that case, worldly things choke out the gospel.

The responses presented so far may leave us with a negative feeling. There are going to be people who totally resist, people who appear to grow quickly, and people who try to hold on to both worldliness and God at the same time. There are those who come to church but never become committed. There is the person who says that he is a Christian, but isn't faithful in his marriage relationship. There is the person who lives his whole life for personal gain, prestige, and money. Those people allow the seed to germinate, but eventually it gets choked out. We've all seen people like that.

The Lord says we're going to have to expect those kinds of responses. What Jesus said here was all prophetic—that is exactly what we see in the church age today. You say, "Maybe those people lost their salvation." Jesus, however, is saying that those people were never saved. The mark of salvation in this parable is that the seed bear fruit. In John 15:2, 6 it says that if you don't bear fruit, God cuts you from the Vine (Christ) and sends you to hell.

A true believer will manifest fruit—that's the mark of salvation.

That takes us to the last soil:

d) The fruitful hearer (v. 23)

"But he that received seed in the good ground is he that heareth the word, and understandeth it ['receive it,' Mark 4:20; 'hold it fast,' Luke 8:15 NASB*], who also beareth fruit, and bringeth forth, some an hundredfold, some sixty, some thirty."

(1) The promise

That soil is very productive. It is bearing three thousand percent, six thousand percent, and ten thousand percent yield on the seed. The soil here is like the rest of the soil, but it is good because of its preparation—no weeds, no rocks, and no hard surface. That is the climax of the whole parable. The Lord is telling the disciples that there is good soil out there. Isn't that a wonderful promise? We have all met hardhearted people, and it's easy to become discouraged by them. Sometimes we'll meet the person who initially appears to be growing fast, but when we see him fall away, we become frustrated. Other times we'll invest our lives in someone who never let the world go, and when we see him fade away, we wonder if it's worth it to share the gospel. But the Lord promises here that there is good soil out there. We're to be faithful and keep sharing the gospel.

(2) The product

(*a*) Manifest

The ultimate mark of salvation is fruitfulness. What is fruit? It's evidence of the divine life. Paul said that the fruit of the Spirit is "love, joy, peace, long-suffering, gentleness, goodness, faith, meekness, self-control" (Gal. 5:22–23). In other words, when you look at a person who is saved, you will see all of those attitudes manifest on a continuous basis. In Paul's writings to the Colossians, Thessalonians, and Philippians, we learn that a saved person is to have the fruit of righteous behavior—the right kind of attitudes and deeds. Paul tells us in Romans that fruit is winning people to Jesus Christ: "I purposed to come unto you . . . that I might have some fruit among you also, even as

---

New American Standard Bible.

among other Gentiles'' (Rom. 1:13). Fruit is God producing spiritual reality in a person's life and is manifest in the attitudes and actions of a person. You show me a person who has no manifestation of fruit, and I'll show you somebody who's going to die out. Fruit is the issue.

Psalm 1 says that a true believer is "like a tree planted by the rivers of water, that bringeth forth its fruit in its season" (v. 3). Fruit is always the mark of true faith. In John 15, Jesus speaks of Himself as the Vine and those in Him as the branches, and says that only the true branches bring forth fruit (v. 5). In Ephesians 2:10, Paul says you are created "unto good works." God already ordained that you produce those works. Now, just because you're to produce fruit doesn't mean you'll never do something wrong; it means that you'll have a consuming desire to be productive—to let God produce through your life. A true believer, when he fails God, will have a great brokenness of heart over the failure because his desire is to see God at work in his life.

(*b*) Multiplied

Notice that Jesus said there will be some who bring a hundredfold, some sixtyfold, and some thirtyfold. This indicates that not everybody is equally productive. God uses people in different ways. There are also some Christians who go through life yielding thirtyfold, when they could be yielding sixtyfold or a hundredfold. Not all Christians will be as fruitful as they could be. When a Christian is disobedient, he restricts the fruitfulness of his life.

I must add, too, that in this parable, Jesus starts at thirtyfold, and that is three times the normal fruitfulness of grain. That tells us that you don't have to scrounge around looking behind the leaves to find a piece of fruit hanging somewhere. A true believer is one whose fruit is multiplied and manifest. The parable shows that a true believer will at least have tremendous and obvious fruit (yielding thirtyfold) and is capable of producing fruit beyond comprehension (yielding a hundredfold). True believers, according to God's plan, are to produce fruit.

What is the Lord teaching in this parable? There are some lessons here for us. First, He is saying, "Go preach the gospel. Realize that as you preach, you'll encounter those who resist, those who appear to be converts but will fall away, and those who are double-minded and can't let go of the world. But you're also going to get true converts. Remember that while you preach, you're going to have an enemy. He is "the wicked one" (Gk., *ho ponēros*, "Satan" [v. 19]). He's going to do everything he can to keep people from becoming converted." Second, in verse 21, He says that there will be people who won't be able to bear the tribulation and persecution of being a Christian. They'd rather be comfortable without any complications in their lives. They're not willing to make the sacrifice required in becoming a Christian. The flesh is an enemy to the gospel. Finally, in verse 22, He says that "the care of this age, and the deceitfulness of riches, choke the word." Thus, there are three constant enemies of the gospel: the devil, the flesh, and the world. They will be trying to stop you as you sow the seed.

Conclusion

There are two basic lessons we can learn in conclusion.

A. The Requirement for Self-Examination

What kind of soil are you? That's the key question Christ is posing here. God help you to be the good ground! If you're the hard ground that the birds snatch the seed from, ask God to plow your heart. If you're the rocky soil underneath a soft, superficial exterior, ask God to plow deeper into your heart. If you're the weedy soil, ask the Lord to clean you so you can receive the gospel with purity. Christ is asking you to look at your own life and see what kind of ground you are.

B. The Requirement for Self-Confidence

The second lesson is this: The issue in the parable is not the talent of the sower. Suppose a little barefoot kid, five years old, wanted to go out and sow a field with his father. His father is able to sow beautifully—he throws the seed with precision. The inexperienced kid is just throwing seed all over the place. Now, the kid may not have as much of his seed hit the good soil as the father's seed, but when the seed hits the good soil, it doesn't matter who threw it. It's going to grow. The response of the soil does not depend on the talent of the sower.

Some people say, "I'd like to preach the gospel and witness for the Lord, but I'm not very talented." That isn't the issue. If you have the seed (the Word of God), then just throw it! I'm always amazed to hear people say, "If so-and-so ever became saved, he could be a great soul winner!" However, Jesus teaches here that it's not the talent of the sower but the nature of the soil that matters. The more seed you throw, the better the chance you're going to hit some good soil. Don't just let out a seed or two a year. Keep slinging the seed, and you'll be amazed at how much good soil is lying around—no matter how incapable a sower you are!

Remember this, too. Sometimes the Lord will plow up the ground that didn't receive the seed when it was first thrown. In fact, in Palestine, sometimes the farmer would throw the seed first, then plow it under afterwards. In the same way, sometimes you'll throw the seed, and before the birds can eat it, the Holy Spirit will plow it under. Hard soil, rocky soil, and weedy soil may not always stay hard, rocky, or weedy. Be faithful and keep throwing the seed in the same field, because God, in His grace, may someday do some tilling in that soil.

The lessons to be learned from this parable are very clear. Examine your life, see what kind of soil you are, and make sure that you're following the Lord Jesus and sowing the seed.

Focusing on the Facts

1. Describe the supernatural capability Jesus had in telling parables (see p. 33).
2. Describe how a sower went about sowing a field in Jesus' time (see pp. 33-34).
3. What are the four kinds of soil that a seed can fall on (see pp. 34-35)?
4. What two purposes did the narrow paths between the fields serve? How do the paths fit in into the parable (see p. 34)?
5. Describe the wayside soil. What two things happened to the seed that landed on this soil (see p. 34)?
6. Describe the stony soil. What initially happened to the seed that landed on this soil? What ultimately happened (see pp. 34-35)?
7. What was deceptive about the weedy soil? Why did the weeds grow so readily? Why must grain be cultivated? What happened to the grain in weedy soil (see p. 35)?
8. Describe the good soil. What kind of crop did good soil normally yield? What kind of crop is indicated by the hundredfold, sixtyfold, and thirtyfold yields (see p. 35)?
9. What did Jesus mean when He said, "Who hath ears to hear, let him hear" (see p. 36)?
10. What does the sower represent in the parable of the sower? Where do we find support for that answer (see p. 36)?
11. What does the seed represent in that parable? If we receive and pass on Christ's message, what are we (see pp. 36-37)?
12. What would happen if we had no seed? Why? What are we to do with the seed (the Word of God) that has been given to us (see p. 37)?
13. Are the soils described in the parable basically the same? Explain (see p. 37).
14. What does the soil refer to (see p. 37)?

15. How did Jesus want the apostles to approach the ministry (see p. 38)?
16. How is salvation manifested (see p. 38)?
17. Describe the attitude of the wayside hearer to the gospel. According to Proverbs and Psalms, what are the characteristics of a man like the wayside hearer (see pp. 38-39)?
18. How does Satan blind people (see p. 39)?
19. What is the immediate response to the gospel by the stony hearer? Is that an external or internal response? Explain (see pp. 39-40).
20. What causes the stony hearer to fall away? Explain how that can happen (see p. 40).
21. What two effects do trouble and persecution have on the church (see p. 42)?
22. What things are in the heart of the weedy hearer? Can someone hold on to both Christ and the things of the world? Use Scripture to support your answer (see pp. 42-43).
23. By mentioning the good soil, what is the Lord telling the disciples (see pp. 44-46)?
24. What is fruit? In what ways is it manifest in a person's life (see p. 44)?
25. Does the fact that we're to bear fruit mean that we will never do anything wrong in our lives? Explain your answer (see p. 45).
26. What is implied by the differences in yields in verse 23? How can we restrict our yield (see p. 45)?
27. What are the three enemies we will face as we sow the gospel (see p. 46)?
28. The issue of the parable is not the talent of the sower. What is the issue? What does that tell us (see p. 46)?

Pondering the Principles

1. The parable of the sower and the seed describes soil in four different conditions. Although the parable talks about whether a person receives or rejects Christ, let's carry the idea of the different soil conditions a little further. As a Christian, are you still the soft, clean, deep soil that you were when you accepted Christ? Or have you recently been allowing your heart to become calloused? Do you find yourself giving in to sin more frequently? Have you been slowly decreasing the amount of time you spend with the Lord in your daily devotion? Have you noticed a decrease in your desire to learn from the Lord's Word? If you have noticed any evidence of your heart becoming more calloused, examine your life and see if your heart needs to be softened. Ask God to give you the desire to be more obedient and to cultivate a deeper relationship with Him through prayer and study of the Word.
2. The stony hearer, who immediately and externally receives the gospel with joy, will fall away when persecution and trouble arises. Second Timothy 3:12 says that all those who are true Christians "shall suffer persecution." Read James 1:2–4. According to verse 2, what should be

our reaction to trials? According to verse 3, what does the testing of our faith produce? If we allow ourselves to be tested by trials, what will be the ultimate result (v. 4)? Just as stringent exercise produces strong muscles, so trials produce strong Christians. Whenever you find yourself under pressure from a trial, thank God for what He is doing in your life, and remember that He is allowing you to go through it for the purpose of making you a mature Christian!

3. Anyone who receives Christ's message (becomes a believer) and passes it on becomes a sower. What kind of a sower are you? Do you take advantage of every opportunity God gives you to share the gospel? Or are you the kind of person who is reluctant to share the message of Christ? Read the following verses: Matthew 28:19; Luke 24:46–48; and Acts 1:8. Jesus commanded the apostles to preach the gospel to every person. In turn, those who accepted Christ through the preaching of the apostles preached to others. Are we today any less responsible to continue the work that Christ first delegated to the apostles? Write down the names of the non-Christians you meet on a regular basis. Pick one or two people out of that list, and ask God to help you make a concentrated effort to take advantage of each opportunity to say something about Christ to those people.

Matthew 13:24-30, 36-43　　　　　　　　　　Tape GC 2300

4
The Kingdom and the World

Outline

Introduction
A. The Curiosity About the Kingdom
B. The Confusion About the Kingdom
　1. The expectation
　2. The explanation

Lesson
I. The Narration
　A. The Parable Declared
　　1. The scene
　　2. The sabotage
　　　a) The time of the attack
　　　b) The technique of the attack
　　3. The surprise
　　4. The solution
　　5. The separation
　B. The People Dismissed
II. The Interpretation
　A. The Characterizations Explained
　　1. The sower identified
　　2. The field identified
　　3. The good seed identified
　　　a) To perfect the saints
　　　　(1) 1 Peter 5:10
　　　　(2) John 16:33
　　　　(3) James 1:2-4
　　　b) To persuade the sinners
　　4. The tares and the enemy identified
　　　a) John 8:44
　　　b) 1 John 3:4-24
　　　c) 1 John 5:19
　　　d) Matthew 5:37
　　5. The harvest time identified
　　　a) An unnecessary condemnation
　　　b) A necessary compassion
　　　　(1) Imitating Christ's patience
　　　　(2) Imposing Christianity's principles

   6. The reapers identified
  B. The Clarification Expressed
   1. The comparison
   2. The condemnation
    a) The gathering together
    b) The casting away
   3. The conversion
III. The Application

Introduction

The Lord Jesus Christ is the ruler of this earth. The Old Testament tells us that God is the King of the universe. "The earth is the Lord's, and the fullness thereof" (Ps. 24:1). In the book of Daniel it was confirmed that "the Most High God ruled in the kingdom of men" (Dan. 5:21). In His kingship over the earth, the Lord Jesus has allowed Satan and sinners a certain amount of freedom. Despite this freedom, He is still the ruling King.

Every phase of human history marks some facet of the rulership of Jesus Christ and God in the world. There is no period of time when the kingdom of God is not in effect on the earth. Initially, God mediated His rule on earth through Adam. Then He mediated His rule through the patriarchs. After that, His rule was successively mediated through the monarchs, the priests and prophets, and the incarnate Lord Jesus Christ. Then, in the early church, God mediated His will and rule through the apostles, by whom God brought revelation to man about His kingdom. There's coming a future time when God will bring His rule to earth through the living, exalted, glorified, incarnate Lord Jesus Christ, in what we know as the millennial kingdom. Finally, after that, the earth and the heaven will be merged in the eternal kingdom, when the universal kingdom and the mediated kingdom on earth will become one.

The Bible clearly delineates all those elements of God's rule on the earth, with one exception—the period of time from the rejection of Christ to the return of Christ. We are living in that age now, and it too is ruled by Jesus Christ. The New Testament designates this form of the kingdom as the mystery form, which was not revealed in the Old Testament. It is through the New Testament teaching of our Lord and the apostle Paul that this age becomes defined for us. Jesus tells us what the character, the extent, the value, and the consummation of this period will be in a series of seven parables in Matthew 13. During this time, God is mediating His rule on the earth through His church, through believers who are indwelt by the Holy Spirit.

  A. The Curiosity About the Kingdom

    The disciples didn't know about this period of time, just as the Old Testament prophets weren't aware of it. Even after Jesus died on the cross, they were still curious about the kingdom. Jesus had taught them much about the kingdom—both before His death and after His resurrection. Their curiosity led them to ask Him "Lord, wilt thou at this time restore again the kingdom of Israel?" (Acts 1:6). Jesus replied, "It is not for you to know the times or the seasons, which the Father hath put in his own power" (v. 7). In other words, it wasn't for them to know when His kingdom would be established. An angel did tell them, however, that "this same Jesus, who is taken up from you into heaven, shall so come in like manner as ye have seen him go into heaven" (Acts 1:11*b*).

B. The Confusion About the Kingdom

1. The expectation

The disciples were told that the kingdom would not come in its fullness until Christ came back. The kingdom of glory, righteousness, and absolute holiness that the prophets anticipated—where the Lord Jesus will rule with a rod of iron and tolerate no evil—will not come until Christ's return. For now, there is a form of the kingdom that is described as "the mystery" (Mark 4:11). That was hard for the disciples to understand; it was a devastating truth to them. They weren't aware of any such form of the kingdom. They didn't know there would be a kingdom that tolerated both good and bad people. They thought that there would be a full and glorious consummation in which the kingdom of righteousness was established and unbelievers were devastatingly judged, punished, cast out, and destroyed. They saw what William Barclay calls "a new and stainless humanity" (*And Jesus Said* [Philadelphia: Westminster 1970], p. 39).

Having already heard the first parable, the disciples probably said to themselves, "There are going to be three kinds of rejecters and one kind of genuine fruit-bearer. What's going to happen to the rejecters?" They may have thought that in Matthew 12 the blasphemous Pharisees who accused Jesus of being Satan were among the rejecters Jesus was talking about. They were probably asking Jesus, "What are You going to do to the rejecters? Are they going to be condemned?" They had good reason to think that, because they knew John the Baptist had said of Christ, "He shall baptize you . . . with fire ["*fire*" being symbolic of judgment]; whose fan is in his hand, and he will thoroughly purge his floor, and gather his wheat into the granary, but he will burn up the chaff with unquenchable fire" (Matt. 3:11*b*–12). John the Baptist, the immediate forerunner of Jesus Christ, didn't even see that interim period. He announced that when Christ came, He would burn the chaff in a fire of judgment and would keep the wheat. That's why the disciples thought that Christ's kingdom would be set up immediately.

The disciples were trying to figure out what would happen to the three kinds of rejecters of Christ. When they ask Jesus in

Acts 1:6, "Lord, wilt thou at this time restore again the kingdom to Israel?" they are really asking, "Is this the time when you're going to condemn those who have rejected You? Is this the time for their devastating judgment?"

2. The explanation

In the second parable, starting with Matthew 13:24, the Lord tells the disciples what He is going to do with the unbelievers who are on the earth during the mystery form of the kingdom. Again, with omniscience, the Lord tells a simple story, the truth of which is infinite. This parable has so many wonderful thoughts in it that I'm just going to have to scratch the surface in trying to explain it. In our study of this parable, we'll be looking at three things: The Narration, The Interpretation, and The Application.

Lesson

I. THE NARRATION (vv. 24–30, 36)

A. The Parable Declared (vv. 24–30)

1. The scene (v. 24)

"Another parable put he forth unto them, saying, The kingdom of heaven is likened unto a man who sowed good seed in his field."

This parable is about the kingdom of heaven. The phrase "the kingdom of heaven" is synonymous with "the kingdom of God." Jesus is talking about the mystery form of the kingdom here. Now, the truth that the parable teaches is true of the age prior to the mystery form of the kingdom and will be true of the millennial kingdom, but Jesus is specifically referring to the mystery form of the kingdom. He says that this form of the kingdom will be like a man who sowed good seed in his field. Notice that this man owns the field that he is sowing—he's not borrowing it. In it, he sows "good seed," not mediocre or average seed.

2. The sabotage (v. 25)

a) The time of the attack

"But, while men slept."

Verse 25 indicates to us that the sower had a crew to help him. He must have been a wealthy man to be able to hire people to help him with the sowing. They were sleeping not because they were lazy, but because it was nighttime. A man who has worked hard has the right to enjoy his sleep.

b) The technique of the attack

"His enemy came and sowed tares [Gk., *zizania*] among the wheat, and went his way."

"Tares," which are also known as *darnels*, are a weedy grass. The enemy came and sowed darnels among the wheat. The word "among" is a very strong Greek expression and indicates that the enemy sowed the darnels all throughout the wheat. After he was finished, he left.

You say, "What is the enemy doing?" One way for a person to destroy the crop of someone he doesn't like is to sow his field full of weeds. In those days, that was done often enough that the Roman government had to have a law against it and prescribe a certain punishment for violaters. It was a great way of ruining your neighbor's crop, and that's exactly what the enemy in that verse did. He secretly oversowed the field with weeds and, having finished his awful deed, went off into the night.

3. The surprise (vv. 26-27)

"But when the blade was sprung up, and brought forth fruit, then appeared tares also. So the servants of the householder came and said unto him, Sir, didst not thou sow good seed in thy field? From where, then, hath it tares?"

The servants who worked for the man were shocked when they saw the darnel growing. They wouldn't have been shocked if there were just a few of those darnels because they were a grassy weed common to the area. There were always a few weeds that had to be dealt with in every crop. The reason they were shocked was because the field was full of weeds.

4. The solution (vv. 28-29)

"He said unto them, An enemy had done this. The servants said unto him, Wilt thou, then, that we go and gather them up? But he said, Nay; lest while ye gather up the tares, ye root up also the wheat with them."

The servants, wanting to save the crop, help their master, and protect their livelihood, asked the master if they should pull out the weeds. When the heads of the crop become mature, the darnels take on a slate gray color, and thus can be differentiated from the wheat. The servants were saying, "We can tell the weeds from the wheat and can go through the field to tear the weeds out." But the master said, "No, don't do that. The darnels are so many, and so close to the wheat, that if you try to pull out the darnels you'll root up the wheat with them."

5. The separation (v. 30)

"Let both grow together until the harvest; and in the time of harvest I will say to the reapers, Gather together first the tares, and bind them in bundles to burn them, but gather the wheat into my barn."

That is a very simple story and easy to understand. But what does it mean? That's what the disciples wanted to know.

B. The People Dismissed (v. 36)

After telling the parable of the wheat and the tares, Jesus told two more parables. Starting in verse 36, Jesus proceeds to explain the parable of the wheat and the tares. We learn from the other gospels that He had to explain all the parables because the disciples could not fully understand them (Mark 4:10-11, 33-34; Luke 8:9-10). But before explaining the parable, we read in verse 36 that "Jesus sent the multitude away." The only people that were left with Him were the disciples. Then He "went into the house [the same house He had left in Matthew 13:1, which was very likely Simon Peter's house in Capernaum (cf. Matt. 8:14)]; and his disciples came unto him, saying, Explain unto us the parable of the tares of the field" (v. 36b). Just as Mark 4:10-11 says, only the apostles and those who were believers got the explanations to the parables. God only revealed His truth to His own.

In the question the disciples asked, notice that they gave a title to the parable, which Jesus hadn't yet done. This shows that they knew the main feature of the story was that the darnels did not belong in the field and that in the end they were going to be burned up. Now that they were alone with Jesus, they asked Him to explain the parable, because they were confused about the form of the kingdom they lived in. Starting in verse 37, Jesus gives them:

II. THE INTERPRETATION (vv. 37-43a)

A. The Characterizations Explained (vv. 37-39)

1. The sower identified (v. 37)

"He answered and said unto them, He that soweth the good seed is the Son of man."

Who is "the Son of man"? Christ is the Son of man. "The Son of man" was a title that Christ used when referring to Himself. In fact, He used it more than any other title for Himself. There was only one time in the New Testament that the phrase was ever used by anybody else to refer to Him (Acts 7:56). He used that title because it identified Him in His incarnation and His humanness. It identified Him as One who lived among us, the perfect man, the second Adam, and the representative of the human race. It is also a Messianic title. In Daniel 7:13 the Messiah is called "the Son of man." It is a marvelous title.

The Jewish leaders knew that it was a Messianic title. In Luke 22:69 Jesus said to the Sanhedrin, "Hereafter shall the Son of man sit on the right hand of the power of God." The Sanhedrin then asked Him, "Art thou, then, the Son of God?" (v. 70*a*). He called Himself "the Son of man," and they asked Him if He was "the son of God." Their response shows that they must have known "the Son of man" was a Messianic reference.

The sower, then, is Jesus Christ. He's the farmer sowing the seed, and He's sowing it in His field.

2. The field identified (v. 38*a*)

"The field is the world."

The Lord is sowing seed in the world, which is His field. He is the sovereign King of the earth. He holds in His hand the title deed to the earth, even though He hasn't really laid claim to it yet as He will as the end of the age when He unrolls the sealed scrolls in Revelation 6 and takes back the earth. Romans 8:22 says "the whole creation groaneth" waiting for Him to take possession of what is rightly His.

So the Lord says that He is sowing seed in the world that belongs to Him. He made the world and planted Adam and Eve in it. Even though Satan came along and usurped everything, the world still belongs to Christ. He created it and will eventually reclaim it.

3. The good seed identified (v. 38*b*)

"The good seed are the children of the kingdom."

This means that the Lord sows the children of the kingdom in the world.

A Frequent Misinterpretation

You would be amazed how complex people have made this parable. Many commentators, in discussing this particular passage, say that the field is the church. They say that both tares and wheat are growing together in the church. But Jesus says here in verse 38 that "the field is the world." That is quite clear, isn't it? You say, "But you have to interpret what He meant when He said that." No, Jesus already made clear what He meant. He said that the field the sower was sowing in represents the world. Some people try to say that "the world" really means the church, and before you know it, someone will come along and say it means the Baptist church, and someone after that will say it means the Baptist church over on a particular street corner. The verse does not say that the field is the church. The Lord said the field is the world. If He had meant that the field was the church, He would have used the word *church*.

If you make the field the church, you will end up with chaos in trying to interpret the parable. For example, when the servants

> ask, "Can we pull out the darnels?" and the Lord says, "Don't pull them out," that would mean we have no right to discipline people in the church or expose a heretic. It would mean that we have no right to deal with sin in the church, whereas in the epistles we are told we can deal with sin in the church. Interpreting the field as the church creates too many problems. Leave it the way the Lord interpreted it—the field is the world.

Jesus is saying that God sows the children of His kingdom throughout the world. The disciples were able to understand that—the mystery form of the kingdom was going to be an earthly one. God is going to plant His people all around the world.

The phrase "the children of the kingdom" is a marvelous phrase. We are the children of the kingdom—the subjects of the Lord Jesus Christ. We have been planted in His world. That is a picture, not of the world in the church, but the church in the world. We who genuinely love the King and affirm His lordship are planted in the world by Him. We're not here by accident. We are planted by the Lord where He wants us. That tells us we're not to be off in a monastery or a holy house or city, away from the world. I know of a man who wanted to build a sinless, holy city and put a wall around it to keep sin out. However, we're not called to isolate ourselves. We've been planted throughout the world and are here for two reasons:

a) To perfect the saints

We have been placed in the world to be matured by the trouble that the world gives to Christians.

 (1) 1 Peter 5:10—"After ye have suffered awhile, [the Lord will] make you perfect."
 (2) John 16:33—"In the world ye shall have tribulation: but be of good cheer; I have overcome the world."
 (3) James 1:2-4—This passage says that the trials we experience in the world mature us and build us up. The Lord plants us in the world to develop us.

b) To persuade the sinners

We have also been placed in the world to influence it. Now, a parable can only go so far before it breaks down as an analogy of spiritual truth, and this is the point where it breaks down, but I still want to introduce this thought. We're in the world to be a good influence for the tares. Everybody who is wheat now was once tares. We were all bad seeds before we were converted. One person said that if you understand verse 38 in a Calvinistic sense regarding predestination, we were planted as good seeds and just grew as good seeds. That's not true. No matter what you believe about predestination, we were all bad from the beginning.

The Lord puts us in the world to be matured by the pressure that it brings and to influence the tares into becoming wheat. Our redemption must be at work in the world. That's why Jesus said to the Father in John 17, "I pray not that thou shouldest take them out of the world, but that thou shouldest keep them from the evil [one]" (v. 15). We're supposed to be in the world.

4. The tares and the enemy identified (v. 38c–39a)

"But the tares [Gk., *zizania*] are the children of the wicked one [Gk., *ho ponēros*, "the devil"]; the enemy that sowed them is the devil."

Satan is called "the wicked one" in several different places in the New Testament. The article "the" is emphatic there, indicating that he is *the* absolutely wicked one, and *the* wicked one of all wicked ones. The very foundation of his being is wretched; he is unmitigated darkness and error personified.

Anybody who is not a child of the kingdom is a child of the wicked one. There are only two kinds of people in the world—children of the kingdom and children of the wicked one. If you're not a child of the King through submission to the lordship of Jesus Christ, then you're a child of the devil. It's that simple. You are on his team, and you are functioning under his control. Ephesians 2 says that the unsaved are directed by the "prince of the power of the air, the spirit that now worketh in the sons of disobedience" (v. 2). That is discussed further in:

a) John 8:44—Jesus said here to the leaders of Israel, "Ye are of your father the devil."

b) 1 John 3:4–24—In this passage of scripture, John contrasts the children of God and the children of the devil. Those are the only kinds of people there are. It is true that there is relative evil within the category of the children of the devil, but they're all representative of Satan himself.

c) 1 John 5:19—"The whole world lieth in wickedness." The whole world lies in the lap of the wicked one.

d) Matthew 5:37—This verse is often overlooked. In Matthew 5, the Lord is contrasting righteous behavior with unrighteous behavior. To sum up a point about what is right, He says at the end of verse 37, "Whatever is more than these cometh of evil." In other words, whatever contradicts or goes beyond God's law proceeds from the evil one. That is a monumental theological statement. The origin of evil is the evil one. God is not the author of evil. The evil one is the enemy who oversowed the good field in the parable

(Matt. 13:25). We see that in creation. God sowed children of the kingdom—Adam and Eve. Then along came the enemy who oversowed, bringing the Fall of man. The sowing and the oversowing have continued through all of human history. Matthew 5:37 tells us that evil comes not from God, but from the evil one.

The Lord sows believers in the world, and Satan oversows his own children in the world. The world, then, is inhabited by both subjects of the King and subjects of the enemy, who is the devil himself. (The word "devil" in verse 39 is the Greek word *diabolos*, which means "enemy or adversary.") This co-mingling has been happening since the Fall and will continue on through the mystery kingdom. In verse 25, when Jesus talked of the enemy who came and sowed tares among the wheat, He used a very strong term that indicates that Satan has sowed his people everywhere. There are some parts of the world where there are nothing but tares. You'd have to look a long time to find wheat in those areas. He has sowed many tares, and he likes to sow them as close to the wheat as he can. He even sows tares in the church. We know that because in Matthew 7:21-23 we read about people who claim to have done good works for Jesus, but the Lord says to them, "Depart from me, ye that work iniquity" (v. 23*b*). Satan has his iniquitous workers sown in the church. The Bible instructs us to throw them out if we find them (Matt. 18:15-17).

In this parable Jesus tells us the way things are going to be in the mystery kingdom. The Judases will be among the apostles. Both exist together, breathe the same air, eat the same food, drive the same highways, live in the same neighborhoods, work at the same factories, go to the same schools, visit the same doctors, entertain themselves with the same entertainment, live under the same sky, and enjoy the same warm sun. Both the just and the unjust receive rain in this era because there will be a co-mingling until the end (Matt. 5:45). That brings us to verse 39:

5. The harvest time identified (v. 39*b*)

"The harvest is the end of the age."

Why does Jesus say that? Because the disciples were ready to put the sickle to the tares. Sometimes we feel like doing the same thing. When we see the wickedness of the world and the grief that it causes to the Lord's church, purposes, and people, we say, "God, why don't you come down and wipe out the world!" David cried the same plea to God, asking God to destroy his enemies (Ps. 13:1-2; cf. Ps. 35). In Revelation 6:9-10 we see under an altar, saints who had been slain, crying out to God, "How long will it be before You judge the earth?" However, through the parable, the Lord is saying, "Don't be impatient; the harvest waits until the end of the age." The phrase "the end of the age" appears several times in Matthew and speaks of ultimate consummation in judgment—that final time when God judges the world (13:39, 40, 49; 24:3, 28:20).

a) An unnecessary condemnation

In verse 28 of the parable, the servants ask the householder, "Wilt thou, then, that we go and gather them [the weeds] up?" The servants are saying, "We can tell the difference between the wheat and the tares, now that they have grown. Do you want us to pull out the weeds?" To that, the lord of the household says, "No, because if you pull out the darnels, you're liable to pull out some wheat, too" (v. 29).

Jesus is simply saying that if we go about trying to judge the world, we're going to end up condemning Christians, because we lack divine insight. God didn't call the church of Jesus Christ to judge the world. He doesn't want us in a position of political power destroying unbelievers, because we don't have the discernment to know who is truly saved and who isn't. It is not the church's function to be pulling out the tares of the world. We have not been called to attack the world. As evidenced by this parable, the wheat and the tares are going to grow together. Satan is going to continue to sow and oversow in the church because he loves to deceive by imitation (2 Cor. 11:13–15). But it is not our responsibility to try to find those tares and rip them out.

You'll notice in history that whenever the church became a political power, it invariably was prone to corrupt its power for the sake of destroying "the apostates." Such was the case in the Inquisition. John Foxe's *Book of Martyrs* tells of many martyrs of Christ who were slaughtered by people claiming to be Christians. During the Crusades, one of the most abysmal periods of human history, crusaders in Europe planned to take the holy places of Israel back from the Turks and, in the process, massacred people all across Europe. They claimed to be doing all of that in the name of Jesus Christ. In one village alone, they trampled three thousand Jewish people with their horses because they said they were apostates.

b) A necessary compassion

(1) Imitating Christ's patience

This is not the age of judgment. What was the Lord Jesus Christ's attitude toward publicans and sinners? He treated them with meekness, love, and kindness. He didn't devastate Judas, even though He knew Judas would betray Him. He was patient, tolerant, and gracious. We are to act the same way. Those of us who are busy trying to destroy the darnels should remember that we too were once darnels. God knows there are still darnels that need time to become wheat. If we go out trying to destroy all the darnels, we put ourselves out of line with God's plan. The Lord knows which people will eventually be in the Kingdom. Speaking of Corinth, God told Paul, "I have many people in this city" (Acts 18:10).

If we as a church act against the ungodly people of the world, then we would be interfering with God, who is patiently waiting for some of those people to come to Him. Our attitude is not to be one of damning the unbelievers of the world and praying that God would destroy them. We're to pray that God would save them. That's the proper attitude. That was the attitude of the Lord Jesus Christ on the night He was betrayed. In John 13:26 Jesus dipped some food and gave it to Judas. Whenever a person did that, he was signifying that the person he gave the food to was an honored guest. Jesus was still showing His love for Judas. We are to act the same way in this age of grace.

We cannot act as executioners. We must be loving, patient, and graciously tolerant like our Lord was. Otherwise, if we try to act in judgment, we might end up destroying the wheat and sparing the rocky and weedy soils. We are to have a heart of compassion, not a heart of condemnation.

(2) Imposing Christianity's Principles

We also cannot apply the spiritual principles that we live by in the kingdom to the rest of the world. You can't say, "I wish worldly people would do what they should do." That's impossible for them, because they're doing the only thing they know how to do—behaving as children of the devil. If you try to enforce Christian standards upon the world, then you are casting your pearls before swine (Matt. 7:6). In the first few verses of Matthew 7, Jesus tells us that we are not to judge one another without carefully examining our own lives: Before we attempt to pull a splinter out of another person's eye, we are to get the two-by-four out of our own eye. Then in verse 6, He says in essence, "Don't do that with the world; that would be casting your pearls before swine." The same could apply to the whole Sermon on the Mount. We are not to take the principles of the Sermon on the Mount and try to enforce them on a society of ungodly people, because they can't apply them. Rather, we are to love them and call them to Christ.

In a sense, we who are saved are in a precarious position because we are co-mingled with the world. But I don't think the Lord is greatly disturbed by that, because the nature of the wheat cannot be changed. We may be next to the darnels, but they can't change our nature. But the converse is not necessarily true; the nature of the darnels can be changed by the influence of godliness. We are called, then, to be patient.

6. The reapers identified (v. 39c)

"And the reapers are the angels."

In the parable, the householder told the servants, "Let both grow together until the harvest; and in the time of harvest I will say to the reapers, Gather together first the tares, and bind them in bundles to burn them, but gather the wheat into my barn" (v. 30). Here in verse 39, Jesus says it is the angels who are called to be reapers. Christians are called only to act as a righteous influence, not to condemn the world. We are to preach against the world's sins, but we are also to love the world's sinners. We are to be gracious and patient with them. We are not God's executioners. If we were, we would end up making terrible mistakes like those that were made in past history.

The Bible says that God is going to judge men at the end of the age, and the angels are going to be the reapers. We see throughout the New Testament, from Matthew to Revelation, that it is the angels whom God has called to reap. Matthew 16:27 says, "For the Son of man shall come in the glory of his Father with his angels." In Matthew 24:31 we are told that "He shall send his angels . . . and they shall gather together his elect." The gathering of those to be judged will be done by the angels. In Revelation 14:15–19 and 19:14, we see that angels are God's agents of judgment. Jesus is saying through the parable, "You are the sowers. I'll have the angels do the reaping."

B. The Clarification Expressed (vv. 40–43a)

1. The comparison (v. 40)

"As, therefore, the tares are gathered and burned in the fire, so shall it be in the end of this age."

We have to wait until the King comes back with His angels before the reaping can occur. Second Thessolonians 1:7-9 confirms this. "When the Lord Jesus shall be revealed from heaven with his mighty angels, in flaming fire taking vengeance on them that know not God, and that obey not the gospel of our Lord Jesus Christ; who shall be punished with everlasting destruction from the presence of the Lord, and from the glory of his power." You say, "When is that going to happen?" "When he shall come to be glorified in his saints" (v. 10). When Christ comes to be glorified in His saints, that's when He will bring His holy angels and burn all the children of the wicked one in unquenchable fire.

2. The condemnation (vv. 41-42)

   a) The gathering together (v. 41*a*)

   "The Son of man shall send forth his angels, and they shall gather out of his kingdom."

   The word "kingdom" refers to the whole world, which is His field. The angels will pull in the net and gather everyone together. Augustine says that the people in that gathering "are like unclean animals in the same ark with the clean, goats in the same pasture as sheep, bad fish in the same net with good ones, chaff on the same floor as grain, vessels to dishonor in the same house with vessels to honor."

   b) The casting away (vv. 41*b*-42)

   "All things that offend, and them who do iniquity [or 'lawlessness' (cf. Mt. 7:23)], and shall cast them into a furnace of fire; there shall be wailing and gnashing of teeth."

   There is coming an inevitable judgment when the Lord will send His angels and pull out of the kingdom all of those who offend Him. All of those who are sinful and unbelieving will be thrown into a furnace of fire.

   A death by fire is the most horrible that a man could ever experience. Fire is the imagery of eternal hell. It speaks of the terrible and everlasting doom of the unrighteous sons of Satan. We read in the Scripture about the burning of weeds (Matt. 13:30), chaff (Matt. 3:12), barren branches (John 15:6), and trees (Joel 1:19). The idea is that the ungodly will be consumed in fire. That is also pictured by the lake of fire in Revelation 19:20, the unquenchable fire in Mark 9:43-48, and the everlasting fire in Matthew 25:41. It is the same fire of Malachi 4:1 and is alluded to in Daniel 12:2. The reaction of the people who will be cast into this fire will be "wailing and gnashing of teeth."

Some people think that hell is going to be fine. They are going to be there with their friends, and they will love it. But Matthew 13:42 tells us that there is going to be grinding of teeth and piercing shrieks. It is going to be a painful, eternal, inescapable judgment. The Lord is saying to the disciples, "Be patient for now and be a good influence during this age. The judgment will come later."

Let's look now at what will happen after the judgment.

3. The conversion (v. 43*a*)

"Then shall the righteous shine forth as the sun in the kingdom of their father."

After the judgment is over, the anticipated kingdom will come. The righteous *Shekinah* will come at that time, lighting the faces of all the saints for all the ages. They will "shine forth as the sun in the kingdom of their Father." In Daniel 12:3 the Bible says the righteous will shine as the stars. They'll shine like the brightness of God's glorious, marvelous heaven.

III. THE APPLICATION (v. 43*b*)

"Who hath ears to hear, let him hear."

You say, "What does that mean?" Jesus is simply saying, "You'd better listen!" Jesus is asking each one of us to look at our own life and ask ourselves, "Am I wheat? Am I a child of the kingdom? Or am I a tare and a child of the enemy?" If you are a child of the enemy, then listen. This is a time of patience and grace. but God's judgment is inevitable, eternal, and painful.

If you are a child of the kingdom, then Jesus has a message for you too. You are to be used by God to influence the darnels near you to become wheat. You are not to condemn the world; that is God's business. Love the sinner and condemn only his sin. Are you being a good influence in the world and persuading the darnels to come to God for salvation?

Focusing on the Facts

1. Why did the disciples think that Christ's kingdom was going to be established immediately? What statement by John the Baptist seemingly supported their belief (see p. 52)?
2. What does the Lord explain in the second parable in Matthew 13 (see p. 53)?
3. In the parable of the wheat and the tares, what form of the kingdom did Jesus refer to (Matt. 13:24; see p. 53)?
4. What are tares? In Matthew 13:25, what does the word "among" indicate about the way the enemy sowed the tares (see p. 54)?

5. What reaction did the servants of the householder have when the crop began to ripen? Why (Matt. 13:26-27; see p. 54)?
6. According to Matthew 13:28, what did the servants want to do? Why did the master not want the servants to do that (Matt. 13:29; see p. 54)?
7. What did the master say he would do to rid the wheat of the tares (Matt. 13:30; see p. 54)?
8. What did the question the disciples asked in Matthew 13:36 reveal about their understanding of the parable (see p. 55)?
9. Who is the sower in the parable (Matt. 13:37)? What significance does the title "the Son of man" have (see p. 55)?
10. What does the field represent (Matt. 13:38*a*; see p. 56)?
11. Who are the good seed (Matt. 13:38*b*; see p. 56)?
12. How is Matthew 13:38*a* commonly misinterpreted? What problem is there with that misinterpretation (see pp. 56-57)?
13. Should Christians hide themselves from the world? Support your answer (see p. 57).
14. What is the first reason God has placed Christians in the world? What is the second reason? What did Jesus say in His prayer to God in John 17:15 (see pp. 57-58)?
15. Who are the tares? Who plants the tares? What does the article "the" in "the wicked one" indicate about Satan (Matt. 13:38*c*; see p. 58)?
16. Into what two categories can the people of the world be placed? If a person is not subject to Christ's lordship, what category does that person automatically fall into (see p. 58)?
17. From whom or what does evil originate (see pp. 58-59)?
18. Satan sows tares in the church. How do we know that (Matt. 7:21-23; see p. 59)?
19. Why did Jesus emphasize to the disciples the fact that the harvest will take place at "the end of the age"? What does the phrase "the end of the age" refer to (Matt. 13:39*b*; see pp. 59-60)?
20. Why are we to allow the wheat and the tares to grow together in the world (see pp. 60-61)?
21. Describe the attitude of Christ toward sinners. What attitude are we to have toward them (see pp. 60-61)?
22. Why can't we apply spiritual principles to worldly people? Rather than imposing Christianity's principles on ungodly people, what are we to do (see pp. 61-62)?
23. Who are the reapers in the parable (Matt. 13:39*c*)? What other scriptures show that to be true (see p. 62)?
24. What kind of people will the angels remove from the kingdom (Matt. 13:41)? Where will those people be placed, according to Matthew 13:42? What will be their reaction to that place (see p. 63)?

25. According to Matthew 13:43a, what will happen to believers after the final judgment (see p. 64)?
26. What did Jesus mean by the phrase "Who hath ears to hear, let him hear" (Matt. 13:43b; see p. 64)?

Pondering the Principles

1. The parable of the wheat and the tares illustrates a great truth: God has planted His children in the world on purpose. We are not to isolate ourselves from the world. Read the following verses: Psalm 145:11–12; Matthew 5:13–16; Acts 1:8; 1 Peter 3:15. What common exhortation is made in all of those verses? As a child of the kingdom, are you influencing the darnels around you as you live your life? Do you find yourself deliberately avoiding any contact with non-Christians? Write down the above verses and place your list where you will see it every day this week. Whenever you find yourself avoiding contact with non-Christians, ask God to give you courage that will enable you to "give an answer to every man that asketh you a reason of the hope that is in you" (1 Pet. 3:15).

2. Christ knows that we face persecution from the world. Memorize John 16:33b for the times that you will need to be comforted when facing that persecution. "In the world ye shall have tribulation; but be of good cheer; I have overcome the world."

3. Make a list of the non-Christians you are in contact with every day. How do you feel toward each person on your list? Do you feel any resentment, impatience, anger, or bitterness toward anyone? How do you think Christ would feel toward each of those people? Think of the different ways that Christ showed His love for the unsaved in the New Testament. Do the unsaved people around you know that you care about them? If so, how do you make your care known? If not, what are some specific things you can do to change that?

Matthew 13:31-32　　　　　　　　　　　　　　　　　GC 2301

5
The Power and Influence of Christ's Kingdom—Part 1

Outline

Introduction
A. The Expectation
B. The Explanation
   1. In the first parable
   2. In the second parable
   3. In the third and fourth parables

Lesson
I. The External Power of the Kingdom
   A. The Instruction
      1. The parable introduced
      2. The potential illustrated
         a) The dispute about the small beginning
            (1) Specified
            (2) Solved
         b) The dispute about the end result
   B. The Interpretation
      1. The commencement
         a) Explained
         b) Exemplified
      2. The culmination
         a) Psalm 72:8-11
         b) Isaiah 54:2-3*a*
      3. The custodianship
         a) Earth's kingdoms
            (1) The Babylonian kingdom
            (2) The Assyrian kingdom
         b) Christ's kingdom

Introduction

In Matthew 13, our Lord gave a series of parables that teach us about the kingdom of heaven. Continuing in our study, let's read verses 31-33, where two more parables appear. The nature of those two parables requires that they be understood together: "Another parable put he forth unto them, saying, The kingdom of heaven is like a grain of mustard seed, which a man took, and sowed in his field; which, indeed, is the least of all seeds; but when it is grown, it is the greatest among herbs, and becometh a tree, so that the birds of the air come and lodge in the branches of it. Another parable spoke he unto them, saying, The kingdom of heaven is like leaven, which a woman took, and hid in three measures of meal, till the whole was leavened."

Small things, ultimately, can have every large effects. All music—symphonies, concertos, oratorios, hymns, and songs—comes from eight notes. All the profound words in the English language come from twenty-six letters. Lord Kelvin once did an experiment to demonstrate that small things can have extensive results. In his lab he suspended a large piece of steel weighing many pounds. He then systematically threw pea-sized wads of paper at the steel. At first, the gentle taps had no effect at all. Eventually, however, the piece of steel was swaying back and forth because of the relentless tapping of the little pieces of paper. The cumulative effect of small things can have profound results. That is the lesson of the two parables in Matthew 13:31–33.

    A. The Expectation

    The disciples believed that Jesus was the Messiah. *Messiah* means "anointed one." He was the Son of David, and the promised King who would set up the kingdom. The disciples expected that kingdom to come in glory and power, accompanied by cataclysmic events and the punishment of evildoers. They anticipated the music, horses, triumph, wonder, and blazing display of majesty and might that was to come when Messiah established His kingdom.

    When things were not happening as the disciples expected, they began to wonder, "Is Jesus the Messiah?" Even though Jesus continually assured the disciples that He was the Messiah, they still struggled with the issue. Even into the book of Acts, we still see them asking Jesus, "Lord, wilt Thou at this time restore again the kingdom to Israel?" (Ac. 1:6b). Because of their expectations, it took them a long time to realize that the Kingdom would come later.

    The disciples thought the Old Testament prophets had prophesied that when the Lord came, all of those who rejected God would receive the full fury of His judgment, and then the Kingdom would come. The disciples became confused because it seemed that those who rejected God kept increasing in number and were becoming more violent and confrontive. Instead of Jesus talking about what He would do to them, He started talking about what they would do to Him. When He said, "They are going to kill Me," the disciples couldn't believe it. When Jesus said, "I must die," Peter said, "Lord, don't let that happen!" (Mt. 16:21–22). When Jesus entered the city of Jerusalem just before His death and people laid palm branches at His feet, crying, "Hosanna to the Son of David," it seemed like that might be when Christ would bring the Kingdom (Mt. 21:8–9). The disciples were probably filled with anticipation at that time, but when the excitement came to its peak, Jesus said, "Verily, verily, I say unto you, Except a grain of wheat fall into the ground and die, it abideth alone." (Jn. 12:24a). He started to talk about His death again.

The disciples were looking for a kingdom of glory, power, majesty, and worldwide wonder, that immediately destroyed rejecting unbelievers. But it didn't come, and Jesus explains why in Matthew 13.

B. The Explanation

Jesus told the disciples, "Before the kingdom comes, there is a form of the kingdom that exists now that you must understand." Jesus refers to that form of the kingdom as the mystery form in Matthew 13:11. That means it was something that was not revealed in the Old Testament. Throughout the seven parables in Matthew 13, Jesus tells the disciples about the mystery kingdom that was to precede the millennial blaze of glory that they were anticipating. Let's look at the first aspect of Jesus' explanation.

1. The first parable

The first parable Jesus tells His disciples concerns four kinds of soil (hearts). Three of them do not receive the message of the King. That indicates that the mystery form of the kingdom includes rejecters. We still have rejecters today. In fact, most of the world is like the hard soil that doesn't let the message in, the rocky soil that accepts it for a little while then falls away from it, or the weedy soil that eventually chokes it out because of the love of worldly things. The Lord says that during the mystery form of the kingdom, He will still be the King and sovereign over the earth, but He will also allow people to reject His message.

Knowing that there would be rejecters in the mystery form of the kingdom, the immediate question that would come into the minds of the disciples was, "What's going to happen to the blaspheming rejecters? What are we to do with them?" Because Jesus was their King and they were His loyal subjects, they were thinking that they should destroy anybody in their society who was a revolutionary. The Lord answers that question.

2. The second parable

In the parable of the wheat and the tares—the kingdom citizens and the rejecters—Jesus says, "The wheat and the tares are going to grow together until the judgment." Jesus made clear that we are not to be the executioners; the angels will take care of the rejecters at the judgment time. Our job is to be the wheat in the midst of the world so that we will influence the tares around us to become wheat. We are not to try to pull the tares out of the ground, or we're likely to harm some Christians in the process and overlook some non-Christians because we don't know the true condition of people's hearts. We are simply to evangelize and let the tares and the wheat grow together.

The disciples were probably thinking by now, "The kingdom is going to be full of rejecters? That's going to be bad, because according to the parable of the wheat and the tares, evil is going to be everywhere because it was sown throughout the field. Will evil choke out the life of the kingdom? Will it strangle the power of Christ in the world?" Christ answers those questions.

3. The third and fourth parables

It is natural that the disciples would be overwhelmed by the thought of so many evil people in the world. They were thinking, "We're the only ones that make up the kingdom of God in the world. The odds are unbelievable. Aren't we going to be destroyed?" In response to that, Jesus taught two more parables and showed the disciples that the kingdom will have a very small beginning. In spite of the opposition, it will ultimately influence the whole world.

The first two parables talk about the conflict. They talk about the antagonism of good and evil in the kingdom—the battle of right and wrong. But the next two parables talk about the victory of good. The third parable speaks of a little mustard seed that will fill the earth, and the fourth parable tells of a little piece of leaven that will permeate the whole loaf of bread. What started out very small will ultimately have a profound influence on everything. Jesus starts Matthew 13 with two parables that describe the nature of the kingdom (believers and nonbelievers side by side) and goes on to two parables that describe the power of the kingdom.

There is another way of looking at the first four parables. The first parable basically talks about the breadth of the kingdom. The seed is sown in the field, and the field represents the world—that is the breadth of the kingdom. The second parable talks about the length of the kingdom. It will go on until the harvest. The third parable, which is about a mustard seed, talks about the height (or extent) of the kingdom. The parable of the leaven talks about the depth of the kingdom. It is hidden in the dough of the world but will eventually influence it. The kingdom is described in those four parables in its breadth, length, height, and depth. The Lord describes it in every dimension. After that, the next two parables talk about the appropriation of the kingdom in the life of an individual. There is a marvelous progression of thought in the parables.

The Lord does not explain the parables of the mustard seed and the leaven to us, but He did give us somebody to explain them. That somebody is the Holy Spirit. We know that Jesus explained the parables to the disciples, because the Bible tells us He explained all of the parables to them. We have the resident Holy Spirit, who helps us to understand the mind of God as revealed in the Word of God and therefore enables us to understand the parables along with the other things we know about God's plans.

Lesson

I. THE EXTERNAL POWER OF THE KINGDOM (vv. 31-32)
   A. The Instruction
      1. The parable introduced (v. 31)

      "Another parable put he forth unto them, saying, The kingdom of heaven is like a grain of mustard seed, which a man took, and sowed in his field."

      This parable is about a farmer who plants a crop of mustard. Mustard was used in those days for many things. It was mainly used for oil, medicinal purposes, and flavoring. Today, mustard seed is a valuable commodity. The producers of Kodak film grow mustard seed to feed to the animals they raise. There is a substance produced in animal bones that, when put together with the silver in the film, will react better with the silver if the animal was fed mustard seed. A number of interesting tests were done that proved that film produced from animals that had been fed mustard seed was better than other films. Mustard seed is still raised as a crop today.

      2. The potential illustrated (v. 32)

      "Which, indeed, is the least of all seeds; but when it is grown, it is the greatest among herbs, and becometh a tree, so that the birds of the air come and lodge in the branches of it."

      The particular mustard seed being spoken of here, when it grows, becomes a bush or shrub. Normally, it grows to a height of seven or eight feet, which is a good-sized garden plant. Mustard is a large herb (Gk., *lachanon*, which is in the herb family). Occasionally, it will grow to a height of twelve to fifteen feet. There are many eyewitnesses that have testified to the fact that mustard plants grow as high as fifteen feet. One writer said that they can grow higher than a person on a horse, and another writer said that a horse and its rider could ride under the branches of some mustard bushes.

      In this parable, the Lord is emphasizing that there is no connection between the smallness of a seed and the largeness of the end result. The small mustard seed can become a very large bush. You can plant a barley seed and get a barley plant of fairly good size. You can plant a seed of wheat or corn and get a good-sized plant. But if you plant a mustard seed, you can get a bush big enough to ride a horse under! That points out the fact that this parable is not an exaggeration. None of the parables are exaggerations; they speak of realities that were known by the people Jesus was speaking to.

a) The dispute about the small beginning

  (1) Specified

In verse 32, Jesus says that the mustard seed "is the least of all seeds." That statement has stirred much controversy. Critics who want to attack the Bible pounce on the statement. They say, "That proves the Bible is not inerrant, because a wild orchid seed is smaller than a mustard seed! Therefore, Jesus didn't know what was truly the smallest seed. If He didn't know that, then He is not God. Or He accommodated the parable to the people's ignorant belief that the mustard seed was in fact the smallest seed." When Bible critics find something they believe to be false in the Bible and say it was written to accommodate what people at that time thought was true, they call it biblical or cultural accommodation. The danger with that is, who can say when something is true and something is false?

The critics say, "Jesus was wrong. He was wrong either because He was ignorant of the truth or because He went along with the ignorance of the people. Either way, He was still wrong." But I think Jesus was right, and I think we can prove it too.

  (2) Solved

The words "grain" in verse 31 and "seeds" in verse 32 are translations of the Greek word *sperma*. The usage of the word "seeds" here refers to seeds sown in an agricultural manner. It refers to seeds planted intentionally. The word "herbs" in verse 32 (Gk., *lachanon*) refers to garden vegetables that are grown specifically for the purpose of being eaten. The same word is used in Roman 14:2 to mean the same thing. It refers to that which is planted as a crop to be eaten as opposed to something that grows wild. The seed referred to in the parable, then, is a seed that was sown agriculturally to produce something edible.

Of all the seeds that were sown at that time in the East and all the seeds that are sown today to produce edible products, the mustard seed was and still is the smallest. In the context Jesus used, what He said was absolutely correct. That was recently affirmed by Dr. L. H. Shinners, the director of the herbarium at Southern Methodist University in Dallas, That herbarium is the largest in the southwest, with 318,000 botanical specimens from all over the world. Dr. Shinners is also a regular lecturer at the Smithsonian Institution. He said, "The mustard seed would indeed have been the smallest of those likely to have been noticed by the people at the time of Christ. The principal field crops (such as barley, wheat, lentils, beans) have much larger seeds as do . . . other plants which might have been present as weeds. . . . There are various weeds and wild flowers belonging to the mustard, amaranth, pigweed, and chickweed families with seeds as small or smaller than mustard itself, but they would not have been particularly known or noticed by the inhabitants." Those weeds and wild flowers were not planted as a crop.

Isn't it wonderful that when Jesus talked about the mustard seed, He was right? If I can trust Him with facts about the mustard seed, then I can trust Him with facts about eternity. Dr. Shinners also said, "The only modern crop plant of importance with smaller seeds than mustard is tobacco, but that plant is of American origin and was not grown in the Old World until the sixteenth century and later."

When Jesus said that the mustard seed was the smallest seed sown by man, He was right.

b) The dispute about the end result

In verse 32, Jesus says that the mustard seed, "when it is grown, it is the greatest among herbs, and becometh a tree." Bible critics are quick to say, "A mustard plant does not become a tree!" However, Jesus was not talking about a big timber tree here. He was talking about a shrub so large that it had the properties of a tree. Verse 32 identifies one property of a tree. "The birds of the air come and lodge in the branches of it." In other words, birds can live in a mustard bush. The branches are large, like those of a tree. The word "lodge" in verse 32 means "to make a home there" in the Greek. The birds could build a nest and stay. There aren't very many bushes that are strong enough to hold a bird's nest. The mustard bush can grow very large, and botanists say that at a certain time of the year, the branches become rigid and birds build their nests in them. The details of the parable are very accurate!

We must keep in mind that Jesus was speaking proverbially in the parable. He wasn't trying to give a lesson on botany.

Because a mustard seed was the smallest seed a Jewish person ever sowed, mustard seeds become proverbial for something small. One proverbial saying that we have today is, "That person is as wise as an owl." But we don't mean that the smartest thing in the world is an owl. It's just a proverbial saying that is commonly used. In the same way, Jesus used something the Jewish people spoke of proverbially to illustrate His point. He also chose a proverb that was accurate. In using the mustard seed to illustrate a point, the Jewish people spoke of such things as a drop of blood as a mustard seed, a tiny breach of the Mosaic law as being a defilement the size of a mustard seed, or a spot or blemish as small as a mustard seed. Today, the Arabs still talk about faith weighing the amount of a mustard seed. Our Lord even uses the proverb in Matthew 17:20, where He says, "If ye have faith as a grain of mustard seed, ye shall say unto this mountain, Move . . . and it shall move." Jesus, in His parable about the mustard seed, used a proverb used by the Jewish people. In His marvelous, infinite wisdom, He used a proverb that was accurate.

Now that we understand what the parable says, let's find out what it means.

B. The Interpretation
  1. The commencement
    a) Explained

    The kingdom will start small. Can you imagine how important it was to tell the disciples that? They were just a little group of men smothered by oppression, rejection, and blasphemy. They thought, "There are just a handful of us against the whole world." Jesus said, "That's OK. That's the plan. The kingdom will start out small." In fact, it was so small that they didn't even recognize it was there. In Acts 1:6 the disciples ask Jesus, "Lord, wilt thou at this time restore again the kingdom to Israel?" In other words, "Where is the kingdom?" Just as the parable of the mustard seed says, the kingdom at that time was so small that it was imperceptible. Many modern theologians don't see it in the gospel of Matthew either. Luke 17:20 says, "And when he was demanded of the Pharisees, when the kingdom of God should come [the Pharisees were asking Him when He was going to bring the kingdom], he answered them and said, The kingdom of God cometh not with observation." In other words, "You can't see the kingdom of God—not in this form." In verse 21 He goes on to say. "Neither shall they say, Lo here [it is]! Or, lo there [it is]! For, behold, the kingdom of God is in the midst of you." The kingdom is already here, but it's starting out as a very small seed. Just like a little mustard seed has the potential to become a massive bush, so does the small beginning of the kingdom have the potential for a kingdom that extends to the ends of the earth.

b) Exemplified

Think of the circumstances of Jesus' birth. He was born in the manger of a stable with smelly animals and a stable floor covered with manure. He was born in obscurity in a country that was nothing but an infant wriggling in the arms of imperial Rome. Israel was but two districts—Judea and Galilee. They were just dots on the earth, along with Samaria, another small region. Jesus also spent thirty years of His life among uncouth, uncultured, and uneducated people in a town called Nazareth. Think of the disciples. All of them put together wouldn't add up to a mustard seed. They were small, inadequate, inconsequential, unqualified, fearful, faithless, and weak. Yet they comprised the kingdom that was planted. In the breast of that little infant in the manger was eternal life that would burst forth into an eternal kingdom.

That is a marvelous truth because it is not seen in the Old Testament. That is a mystery revealed. The kingdom started with just the little group of disciples. By the time Jesus ascended into heaven in Acts 1:9, there were only about 120 believers (Acts 1:15). There are many more now, and by the time the harvest time comes, the kingdom will cover the entire globe.

2. The culmination

The kingdom started out very small, and it will be very large in the end. That is the basic outline of the parable. When we read what the Old Testament prophets saw regarding the kingdom, we find that its extent will be staggering.

a) Psalm 72:8–11

"He shall have dominion also from sea to sea, and from the river unto the ends of the earth. They that dwell in the wilderness shall bow before him, and his enemies shall lick the dust. The kings of Tarshish and of the isles shall bring presents; the kings of Sheba and Seba shall offer gifts. Yea, all kings shall fall down before him; all nations shall serve him."

That's the extent of the kingdom. That's how big the bush will become. It will have its origin from a little seed—that is what the Lord wants us to understand. The kingdom will have great impact, and all from a small beginning.

b) Isaiah 54:2–3*a*

"Enlarge the place of thy tent, and let them stretch forth the curtains of thine habitations; spare not, lengthen thy cords, and strengthen thy stakes; for thou shalt break forth on the right hand and on the left, and thy seed shall inherit the nations."

The Messiah's kingdom will extend from one end of the globe to the other.

Jeremiah, Amos, Micah, and Zechariah all prophesied about the extent of Jesus' kingdom. There are many passages in the Bible that say that the kingdom of God will stretch from sea to sea, from land to land, and cover the whole globe. Ultimately, the millennial kingdom will come, and Christ will reign over the whole earth. In Revelation 11:15 we read, "The kingdom of this world is become the kingdom of our Lord, and of his Christ, and he shall reign forever and ever."

The parables in Matthew 13 take us into the Millennium—into the fullness of the ultimate growth of the kingdom. No matter how insignificant it appeared and how despised it was, Christ's rule started out small. Those who hated Him probably thought that after He was killed, they were freed of Him. But the kingdom will continue to grow, and its consummation will be amazingly out of proportion to its beginning, much like the contrast between a mustard bush and its seed.

This parable is meant to encourage us. It is easy for us to get discouraged sometimes. We may feel that no matter how hard we try, we always seem to be crushed and crowded out by the evil world around us. If we feel that way, can you imagine how the disciples felt? However, there are many believers all over the world today, and there are still many people coming to Christ. In some countries there are thousands of people coming to Christ every day. The kingdom is growing. But even then, we remember that the battle is intense and that we're still in the minority. Imagine how the disciples felt. Their leader was blasphemed in their presence, and they experienced a sense of hopelessness, defeat, bewilderment, and discouragement. At first, when John the Baptist started preaching, people were flocking out to see him, and everything was exciting. He said of Christ, "He must increase, but I must decrease" (John 3:30). Everyone was becoming excited because they thought the kingdom was about to be established.

Jesus attracted crowds, did miracles and healings, multiplied food, and walked on water. It seemed that the kingdom was coming. But then things began to change. There began to be a mounting hatred and bitterness toward Jesus. People began to reject Him. So to assure the disciples that everything was OK, He told them that the kingdom was going to start out small, but it was going to become big. They were going to win in the end. The kingdom was going to stretch across the face of the earth and go on into eternity.

3. The custodianship

The planted mustard seed, according to the parable, became a tree. The branches were big enough for birds to build their nests on. The question comes up, "What do the birds represent?" Some people think they represent demons and evil. The reason they think that is because the birds in the parable of the soils represented Satan snatching the Word away from people. However, birds don't always represent Satan or evil. In the parable of the mustard seed, they are simply illustrative.

The presence of birds in the mustard plant means that it has large branches. There were other reasons that birds chose to live in a mustard tree. The seeds in the tree are a source of food for the birds (the mother bird won't have to go out hunting for food all the time). The tree also provides shade, protection, and security.

a) Earth's kingdoms

Trees often illustrated kingdoms in the Old Testament.

(1) The Babylonian kingdom

In Daniel 4, Nebuchadnezzar, the king of Babylon, has an interesting dream. A description of the dream starts in verse 10: "Thus were the visions of mine head in my bed: I saw and, behold, a tree in the midst of the earth, and the height of it was great. The tree grew, and was strong, and its height reached unto heaven, and the sight of it to the end of all the earth. Its leaves were fair, and its fruit much, and in it was food for all; the beasts of the field had shadow under it, and the fowls of the heavens dwelt in its boughs, and all flesh was fed from it" (vv. 10–12). Daniel, interpreting the dream for Nebuchadnezzar, said this: "The tree that thou sawest, which grew, and was strong, whose height reached unto the heaven, and the sight of it to all the earth, whose leaves were fair, and its fruit much, and in it was food for all; under which the beasts of the field dwelt, and upon whose branches the fowls of the heavens had their habitation: It is thou, O king, that art grown and become strong; for thy greatness is grown, and reacheth unto heaven, and thy dominion to the end of the earth" (vv. 20-22).

Daniel was saying that the Babylonian Empire had become like a tree, and all of the nations of the world were finding their comfort, security, and food in that tree. Babylon brought culture, education, architecture, prosperity, and a sense of peace to the world. There were many nations (birds) lodging in the tree of the Babylonian Empire.

(2) The Assyrian kingdom

The Assyrian Empire is described in Ezekiel 31:3-6 as a tree. "Behold, the Assyrian was a cedar in Lebanon with fair branches, and with a shadowing shroud, and of an high stature; and its top was among the thick boughs. The waters made it great; the deep set it up on high with its rivers running round about its plants, and sent out its little rivers unto all the trees of the field. Therefore, its height was exalted above all the trees of the field, and its boughs were multiplied, and its branches became long because of the multitude of waters, when it shot forth. All the fowls of the heavens made their nests in its boughs, and under its branches did all the beasts of the field bring forth their young, and under its shadow dwelt all great nations."

Little nations, which need protection, provisions, and security, will often shelter themselves in the branches of dominant world powers. The United States has traditionally and historically been a great tree where other nations have found shelter. For example, it has provided foreign aid and education to other nations.

b) Christ's kingdom

The kingdom of Christ (the mustard bush) is going to grow so big that the nations find their shelter and protection in it. The birds in the mustard bush are not necessarily a part of the kingdom; they just benefit by its presence on earth in the same way that non-Babylonian nations benefited from the presence of the Babylonian Empire. When we talk about the kingdom, sometimes we are specifically referring to the true saints, and other times we are referring to God's sovereign rulership over everything. In the parable of the mustard seed, Christ is referring to God's sovereign rule over all the earth.

Christ is saying, then, that wherever Christianity flourishes, the people who climb in the branches prosper, even though they don't know Christ. America is what it is today because of its Christian heritage. There are many birds in its bush. Not all of them are Christians, but they still receive the benefits. The dignity of life in America, the jurisprudence system, the law, the sense of right and wrong, education, free enterprise, the dignity of women, and the care of children all rise out of Christian truth. Reform movements throughout history have had their roots in biblical truth. Wherever the kingdom's influence is felt, there is an environment of protection for those who aren't even in the kingdom.

Can an Unbeliever Benefit from God's Blessings?

First Corinthians 7:14 is a microcosm of what Matthew 13:32 teaches. Paul says that if a believer is married to an unbeliever, and the unbeliever wants to remain married to the believer, let him stay, because the unbeliever is sanctified in the presence of the believer. An unbeliever married to a believer benefits just by being with somebody receiving the blessings of God. The unbeliever, then, is sheltered by the tree of the believer.

The kingdom of heaven on earth is the same thing, only on a much larger scale. The people who find lodging within that kingdom are the most blessed people in terms of human life.

If you contrast the part of western culture under the influence of Christianity as opposed, for example, to India or an aboriginal part of the world where Christianity has never been, then you can understand what Christ is saying. There will be many who will find lodging in the kingdom's branches.

The Lord is teaching us, then, that in spite of the three bad soils and the darnels, Christians are going to win. The kingdom is going to continue to grow. That's the promise the Lord makes in the parable. Those of us who are Christians are not just a small group of people waiting to be defeated by the world. We're part of a growing kingdom, and we're on the winning side!

Focusing on the Facts

1. Describe the experiment Lord Kelvin did in his lab. What did the experiment prove (see p. 68)?
2. After Jesus told the parable of the wheat and the tares, what were the disciples probably thinking? In response to that concern, what did Jesus show the disciples in the third and fourth parables (see pp. 68-70)?
3. The kingdom of heaven is described in the first four parables in Matthew 13 in its _____, _____, _____, and _____ (see p. 70).

4. What was mustard used for in the time of Christ (see p. 71)?
5. How high do mustard bushes normally grow? How high have some eyewitnesses seen them grow (see p. 71)?
6. What is the Lord emphasizing in the parable of the mustard seed? What does the fact that mustard bushes can become large tell us about the parable (see pp. 71-72)?
7. Jesus said in Matthew 13:32 that the mustard seed "is the least of all seeds." What is the response of Bible critics to this statement? How could you respond to their criticism on that point (see pp. 72-73)?
8. What does the word "seed" in the parable refer to? What does the word "herbs" in verse 32 refer to (see p. 72)?
9. Jesus said that the mustard seed, "when it is grown, it is the greatest among herbs, and becometh a tree" (Matt. 13:32). What is the response of Bible critics to that statement? What did Jesus mean when He called the mustard bush a tree (see p. 73)?
10. What is the significance of the word "lodge" in Matthew 13:32? What does it tell us about the branches of the mustard bush (see p. 73)?
11. We must keep in mind that Jesus was speaking _____ (see p. 73).
12. What are some examples of the ways the Jewish people used the smallness of the mustard seed to illustrate a point (see p. 74)?
13. How did the kingdom of God start out? Was the kingdom on earth during the life of Christ? Use Scripture to support your answer (see p. 74).
14. What fact about the kingdom is revealed to us in Psalm 72:8–11 and Isaiah 54:2–3*a* (see pp. 75-76)?
15. What is the parable of the mustard seed meant to do for us? How does it accomplish that (see p. 76)?
16. What mistake do people commonly make about the birds in the parable of the mustard seed? Why do they make that mistake (see p. 77)?
17. What two kingdoms were symbolized by trees in the Old Testament? What benefits did the nations under those kingdoms experience as a result of being under their influence (see pp. 77-78)?
18. Are all the birds that lodge in the mustard bush a part of the kingdom? Explain (see p. 78).
19. Why is America what it is today? What are some of the benefits in America today that came from biblical roots (see pp. 78-79)?
20. Explain one way an unbeliever can benefit from God's blessings (1 Cor. 7:14). In terms of human life, what is true about the people who find lodging within the current kingdom on earth (see p. 79)?
21. What promise does the Lord make to Christians in the parable (see p. 79)?

Pondering the Principles

1. After Jesus told the disciples the first two parables in Matthew 13, they were feeling overwhelmed by that fact that there would be so many evil

people in the world during the mystery form of the kingdom. Have you ever felt powerless and defeated in the midst of all the evil going on around you? Read John 16:33. Jesus said this to comfort the disciples after He told them He would be leaving them to return to heaven and that they would face persecution. In the last part of the verse, what attitude did Jesus tell the disciples to have? Why? In the beginning of John 16:33, Jesus says, "These things I have spoken unto you, that in me ye might have peace." Before the events of the crucifixion occurred, Jesus told His disciples what would happen, so their hearts would not be troubled. Read John 14:27. What did Jesus promise the disciples? What command did Jesus give at the end of the verse? Philippians 4:6-7 says that we have that same peace. Is your heart troubled by the tribulation you face in the world? Write out the above three verses on a small card and put it in a place where you can look at it frequently. Whenever you look at it, ask God to help you remember the peace that Christ has already promised you!

2. Christ's kingdom is on earth now in the hearts of those who have received Him as their Lord. In the parable of the mustard seed, Christ told the disciples that the mystery form of the kingdom was going to become large and spread all over the earth. What evidence can you see of the growth of Christ's kingdom in the area you live? In what laws can you see the Bible reflected? What activities do you know about that are promoting the gospel in foreign countries? Does thinking about those things help you to get a much broader perspective of the size of Christ's kingdom on earth? Make an effort to keep up with what God is doing in your own community and the different countries of the world. Doing that will help you to remember that Christ's kingdom is still growing, as the parable of the mustard seed said it would. Knowing that Christ's kingdom is growing as Christ promised can be a true encouragement when you feel crushed by the world around you.

Matthew 13:33 GC 2302

6
The Power and Influence of Christ's Kingdom—Part 2

Outline

Introduction
A. The Anticipation
   1. The prophecy of Micah
   2. The prophecy of Zechariah
B. The Affirmation
   1. The nature of the kingdom
   2. The power of the kingdom

Review
I. The External Power of the Kingdom
   A. The Instruction
   B. The Interpretation

Lesson
II. The Internal Power of the Kingdom
   A. The Instruction
      1. The practice
      2. The portion
      3. The pattern
      4. The power
      5. The person
      6. The particulars
      7. The placement
   B. The Interpretation
      1. The influence of the kingdom is great
         a) The clarification
         b) The confusion
            (1) The primary argument
            (2) The proper application
            (3) The prime appropriation
               (*a*) In relation to salvation
               (*b*) In relation to separation
         c) The conclusion
      2. The influence of the kingdom comes from within

Conclusion
A. The statistics
B. The specifics

Introduction

Matthew 13 describes the kingdom of our Lord in the time between His rejection and His second coming. The two parables in Matthew 13:31-33 tell about the influence that the kingdom will have in the world. We looked at the first parable in our last lesson and will look at the second parable now. Let's read the two parables together, because they deal with the same theme. "Another parable put he forth unto them, saying, The kingdom of heaven is like a grain of mustard seed, which a man took, and sowed in his field; which, indeed, is the least of all seeds; but when it is grown, it is the greatest among herbs, and becometh a tree, so that the birds of the air come and lodge in the branches of it. Another parable spoke he unto them, saying, The kingdom of heaven is like leaven, which a woman took, and hid in three measures of meal, till the whole was leavened."

Both parables speak of one theme. They speak about influence. They speak about small beginnings with great conclusions. If you throw a stone in a lake, its influence will touch every shore. The Lord is saying in the parables that the kingdom will start out small, but ultimately, its influence will be global. He is saying that the kingdom will grow to its fruition and fulfillment. Its power will become worldwide, just as God intended.

We live in the time when that is being fulfilled. Never in the history of the world has Christianity had the global influence that it has today. It is amazing to think that Christianity began with a small group of disciples and has become what it is today. But that is exactly what the parables in Matthew 13:31-33 prophesied would happen. The integrity of Jesus Christ and the truthfulness of the Word of God is at stake in the fulfillment of those parables.

A. The Anticipation

In the Old Testament, prophets predicted that the kingdom of God would eventually come to earth and encompass the entire globe. Jesus Christ was to be God's representative—the Son of David, the anointed, the Messiah, the King—who would sit on the throne in the city of Jerusalem and rule the world. In the prophesied coming kingdom, there would be worldwide peace, no crime, no poverty, and the alleviation of suffering and death. There would be salvation among all the nations, as well as among the Jewish people. In the kingdom, Christ will be revered and honored as King; all rebels and blasphemers will be destroyed.

1. The prophecy of Micah

Micah, the prophet, wrote in the fourth chapter of his book, "But in the last days it shall come to pass, that the mountain of the house of the Lord shall be established in the top of the mountains, and it shall be exalted above the hills, and people shall flow unto it" (v. 1). Micah is describing here the kingdom in the last days, when Christ is reigning on the throne and the nations are coming to worship Him and give homage to His rule. Verse 2 continues, "And many nations shall come, and say, Come, and let us go up to the mountain of the Lord, and to the house of the God of Jacob; and he will teach us of his ways, and we will walk in his paths; for the law shall go forth from Zion, and the word of the Lord from Jerusalem. And he shall judge among many people, and rebuke strong nations afar off; and they shall beat their swords into plowshares, and their spears into pruning hooks; nation shall not lift up a sword against nation, neither shall they learn war any more. But they shall sit every man under his vine and under his fig tree [everybody will have his own food and resources], and none shall make them afraid; for the mouth of the Lord of hosts hath spoken it. For all people will walk every one in the name of his god, and we will walk in the name of the Lord, our God, forever and ever" (vv. 2–5). The world will come to the feet of the Messiah, and those who rebel will be rebuked by the Lord. Other prophecies tell us that God will rule His kingdom with a rod of iron through His Son and that justice will be swift and immediate (Ps. 2:8–9; Jer. 23:5).

2. The prophecy of Zechariah

   The eighth chapter of Zechariah has more to say about Christ's kingdom. In Zechariah 8:18–19 we read, "The word of the Lord of hosts came unto me, saying, Thus saith the Lord of hosts: The fast of the fourth month, and the fast of the fifth, and the fast of the seventh, and the fast of the tenth, shall be to the house of Judah joy and gladness, and cheerful feasts." In other words, the fasts will be turned into feasts. Fasts were times of remembering tragic events. For example, the Jewish people fasted in memory of the time they were taken into captivity. The fast of the fourth month, which is mentioned at the beginning of verse 19, commemorated the flight of the royal seed when Jerusalem was taken by Babylon (Jer. 39:2–4). The fast of the fifth month commemorated the destruction of the Temple (Jer. 52:12–13); the fast of the seventh month commemorated the murder of Gedaliah, their governor (Jer. 41:1–2); and the fast of the tenth month commemorated the beginning of the siege by Nebuchadnezzar that led to the captivity (2 Kings 25:1; Jer. 39:1).

   Some Jewish people still celebrate those fasts today. But Zechariah said that the fasts will be turned into cheerful feasts. There is coming a day when there will be no need to remember the sorrowful events of the past. Zechariah 8:20–23 says, "It shall yet come to pass that there shall come peoples, and the inhabitants of many cities; and the inhabitants of one city shall go to another, saying, Let us go speedily to pray before the Lord, and to seek the Lord of hosts. . . . Yea, many peoples and strong nations shall come to seek the Lord of hosts in Jerusalem, and to pray before the Lord. Thus saith the Lord of hosts: In those days it shall come to pass that ten men . . . shall take hold of the skirt of him that is a Jew, saying, We will go with you; for we have heard that God is with you.'' The world is going to come to the Messiah, and the Jewish people will be the agents that bring the world to the feet of Christ. There will be feasts and joy and gladness in the kingdom; the rebels will be purged from it.

The Jewish people lived in anticipation of that kingdom. They expected it to come when Jesus came. But none of the things they expected to happen came to pass. Jesus didn't purge the rebels. He didn't sit on a throne. He didn't overthrow the Romans. There was still war; people weren't beating their swords into plowshares or spears into pruning hooks. There wasn't peace in the world, and there wasn't the punishment and condemnation of those who rejected God. Since the Jewish people didn't see the fulfillment of their expectations when Jesus came, they couldn't believe that He was the King He said He was. Even the people who believed that Jesus was the Messiah struggled with doubts.

B. The Affirmation

There is no question in my mind that Jesus is a King. That's why He was born here on earth. Neither is there any question in my mind that we are living in a kingdom now. It is not a kingdom in the way that men understand kingdoms. It is a kingdom within the heart. That is why in Romans 14:17 Paul says, "For the kingdom of God is not food and drink, but righteousness, and peace, and joy in the Holy Spirit.'' It is an internal kingdom. In Luke 17:20, the Pharisees say to Jesus, "If you're a King, where is the kingdom?'' Jesus said, "Behold, the kingdom of God is in the midst of you'' (v. 21). Even though they couldn't perceive the kingdom, He was still the King.

Now, the disciples believed that Jesus was the King, but they still wondered where the kingdom was. They were still looking for the outward display of the kingdom, especially after having seen Jesus blasphemed in Matthew 12. Jesus then said to the disciples, "I'm going to teach you now about the period of My reign and My kingdom. The full glory of the kingdom will come just as Micah and Zechariah prophesied, but for now, there will be a mystery form of the kingdom (Matt. 13:11). During that time, the kingdom will differ from what it will ultimately be.'' Then throughout Matthew 13, in a series of seven parables, Jesus describes what the mystery form of the kingdom will be like.

1. The nature of the kingdom

    The first two parables describe the nature of the kingdom. The parable of the soils and the parable of the wheat and the tares say that good and evil will coexist in the kingdom. The parable of the soils says that there will be soil that rejects the gospel and soil that accepts it. In other words, there will be people who refuse the kingdom and people who receive the kingdom. The second parable says that good and evil will grow together until the final judgment. We're not to expect rebels to be condemned, devastated, or consumed.

2. The power of the kingdom

    In the parables of the mustard seed and the leaven, Jesus says that in spite of the coexistence of good and evil and the tremendous power of sin and Satan, the power of the kingdom is so great that it is going to grow. Just because three out of four soils will reject the gospel and Satan oversows the wheat with tares doesn't mean the kingdom will be overcome by evil. From a small beginning, like a mustard seed, the kingdom is going to grow. Like a tiny piece of leaven hidden in a massive pile of dough, it will permeate its environment.

    Those two parables are a message of hope. The first two parables told us that God will allow evil to continue in the world. I hate sin. There are many times when I feel like David did. He often cried out for God to destroy sinners and sin. I'm sure there are times when you wish you could act as God's executioner and purge sin. But the first two parables say no, we cannot do that. This is a time of God's grace; judgment will come later. It is distressing to know that we have to tolerate evil, but the third and fourth parables are a message of hope. In spite of the evil, the kingdom is going to grow and fill the earth. I believe that the full grown mustard tree and the permeated dough illustrate the beginning of the Millennium.

    The next two parables also have a common subject. In them, Jesus talks about

3. The appropriation of the kingdom

    The first four parables take a general look at the kingdom, and the next two parables take a specific look at the kingdom. The first two parables speak of the nature of the kingdom, the next two speak of the power of the kingdom, and the two following them speak of the appropriation of the kingdom. That is very important, because when you interpret the parable of the leaven, you want to interpret it in the homiletic consistency that our Lord uses as He progresses in teaching the parables.

The parable of the leaven has been greatly misunderstood by many people. As we study it, I am going to share with you what I think should be made clear about the parable. We've already learned from the parable of the mustard seed that the kingdom will start small but become large, and many nations will benefit from it. The parable of the leaven has a very similar lesson.

Review

I. THE EXTERNAL POWER OF THE KINGDOM (vv. 31-32; see pp. 71-79)

   A. The Instruction (see pp. 71-74)

   B. The Interpretation (see pp. 74-79)

Lesson

II. THE INTERNAL POWER OF THE KINGDOM (v. 33)

   A. The Instruction

"Another parable spoke he unto them, saying, The kingdom of heaven is like leaven, which a woman took, and hid in three measures of meal, till the whole was leavened."

      1. The practice

Our Lord always told parables that portrayed things commonly done by the people He spoke to. While He was growing up, He would have seen His mother make bread many times. He would have seen her using leaven (or yeast, or sourdough) in the process. The person making bread would prepare a batch of dough, knead it, and put a piece of sour, fermented dough from a former loaf of bread in the new loaf. That leaven would cause the new loaf to foment and bubble and would permeate the whole loaf, causing it to rise. Our Lord and the people He was speaking to probably saw that happen countless times.

      2. The portion

The size of the piece of leaven put into the new loaf of bread was very small. But you'll notice in the parable that it was "hid in three measures of meal." That is a massive amount of dough. Three measures of meal is equivalent to an ephah. That means the amount of dough being leavened was large. It was common at that time to prepare large amounts of bread because it was the staple of life, and there had to be enough to feed large families and any servants the families had.

      3. The pattern

When I read about the leaven being put into three measures of meal, I was stunned because an ephah of dough would make an almost inconceivable amount of bread. I did some research and found out that when the Lord and two angels visited Sarah and Abraham (Genesis 18), Sarah used three measures of meal in the bread that she made for them to eat. When Gideon made some bread (Judges 6:19), he also used three measures of meal, or one ephah. Apparently, three measures of meal for bread was a common recipe.

4. The power

    The large amount of meal that a little piece of leaven can influence indicates the enormity of the task that leaven can accomplish. That is parallel to a small mustard seed producing a large mustard bush. A tiny piece of leaven is capable of extending its impact to a massive amount of dough.

5. The person

    Notice that the parable says a woman is making the bread. Women worked outside with the oven in those days, while men worked in the fields. It is still very much the same in many places today.

6. The particulars

    Leavened bread is far superior to unleavened bread. Unleavened bread is flat, hard, dry, and unappetizing. Leavened bread is soft, spongy, and tasty. There are two things to notice about leaven. One, a small amount can influence a massive amount of dough. Two, it influences the dough in a positive way. It makes the bread much better and more tasty.

7. The placement

    The parable says that the woman hid the leaven in the dough. The leaven has to be inserted in the bread. It can't sit on the counter and tell the bread to rise. God didn't extend His influence in the world by standing on a cloud and telling people what to do; He did it by sending Christ. The leaven has to be injected into the bread before it can begin its permeating work. That was something every Jewish person knew about, because everyone was familiar with the process of making bread.

B. The Interpretation

What are the lessons to be learned from the parable? It is a very simple story with very simple lessons, but of all the parables I've studied, it is the one most often misunderstood. Many of you may have never heard the alternative view of the parable before, so I will discuss it here.

1. The influence of the kingdom is great

    a) The clarification

    The power of the kingdom is great. It's like a tiny bit of leaven that influences a great mass of dough. The fact that the kingdom starts out small is not necessarily debilitating because the kingdom has the power to influence everything. The measures of meal (the dough) is like the world. When you plant the kingdom of heaven in the middle of the world, it will eventually influence it, because inherent in the kingdom is a bubbling, fomenting, supernatural power. I believe the leaven represents the good influence of Christ's kingdom—His gospel and His people—in the world.

b) The confusion

Some people think the leaven represents evil. They believe the parable is teaching that evil is going to be in the kingdom and permeating it. But that interpretation doesn't fit with the flow of what Jesus is teaching. In the first two parables, He talks about the evil in the world, and then in the next two parables, He talks about the power of the kingdom overcoming evil. The interpretation that the leaven represents evil is inconsistent with what our Lord is teaching.

In the parable, Jesus says, "The kingdom of heaven is like leaven." It is obvious that the kingdom of heaven is being likened to leaven in the parable. I believe that Jesus is talking about the kingdom of heaven in a positive way. He is saying that its influence makes the word better, in the same way that leaven makes bread better.

(1) The primary argument

Those who believe the leaven represents evil in the parable base their argument on this: Every other time leaven is mentioned in the New Testament, it always refers to evil. Therefore, to be consistent, it must refer to evil here. They say that even Jesus used leaven to refer to evil. I want to take issue with that. Leaven is not intended to refer to evil. You say, "But in Luke 12:1, Jesus said, 'Beware of the leaven of the Pharisees, which is hypocrisy.' "

When Jesus said that, He was not making leaven represent the hypocrisy of the Pharisees; He was making it represent the influence of the Pharisees' hypocrisy. The use of leaven in an analogy is appropriate only when it refers to its permeating influence. The point of using leaven to describe the hypocrisy of the Pharisees was to show that their hypocrisy permeated everything that they did, much in the same way that leaven thoroughly permeates bread.

Leaven is not an illustration of sin; it is an illustration of permeation. That is very important. If you take the analogy any further than that, you will destroy it. When evil is being referred to in the Bible, it is called darkness, blackness, or the absence of light. But when leaven is used to illustrate something in the Bible, it refers to something that permeates.

(2) The proper application

You can't take analogies and absolutize them into theological terms. In other words, leaven only illustrates something; it does not have an absolute, theological meaning. You can't say that whenever the word *leaven* appears in the Bible, it refers to sin. Leaven is only an analogy. If you make it refer to sin, you'll have a lot of trouble. Did you know that in the Old Testament, the Jewish people were commanded to offer God leavened bread at the Feast of Pentecost (Lev. 23:15-21)? If you say that leaven refers to evil, then you are saying that the Jewish people offered evil to God. Therefore, leaven cannot be used as more than a simple illustration.

Leaven is basically used in the New Testament to illustrate permeation. It refers to the permeating effect of different sins, not just hypocrisy. In Galatians 5:9, it is used of legalism. It is used of immorality in 1 Corinthians 5:6-8. Leaven can also be used as an analogy for something that has a good influence. Even though it has never been used anywhere in the New Testament except Matthew 13:33 as an analogy for a good influence, that doesn't mean the Lord can't use it to mean that. You can't extrapolate from the other uses of leaven in the New Testament.

(3) The prime appropriation

(*a*) In relation to salvation

First Corinthians 5 gives us some insight about leaven as a permeating influence. In that passage, Paul indicts the Corinthian church for their sin and uses leaven in his illustration. "Know ye not that a little leaven leaveneth the whole lump?" (v. 6). That is simply a proverbial statement. Paul is saying, "A little thing can have a lot of influence." We have a similar proverbial statement that the Bible doesn't use. One rotten apple spoils the barrel. That analogy goes further, because it starts with a rotten apple, which symbolizes an evil influence. But leaven is neutral. You can apply it any way you want. Leaven makes bread better, but it can be used to speak of anything that begins small and has a massive, permeating influence.

Verse 7 shows how Paul uses the analogy. "Purge out, therefore, the old leaven, that ye may be a new lump." In other words, he's saying to the Corinthians, "You're Christians now. You're each a new lump of dough. Don't put leaven into your new lump." Leaven for a new loaf of bread comes from an old loaf. It was put aside to ferment and then put into a new loaf. Paul is telling the Corinthians that because they are new creatures in Christ, they are not to allow their former lives to influence their new lives. It's a beautiful illustration. Paul is telling them to cut the continuity. They are not to pull a little piece of leaven from the old loaf of bread and use it to start the next loaf. They are to cut off everything from their former lives and start with a brand new loaf of bread.

Verse 7 continues, "For even Christ, our passover, is sacrificed for us. Therefore, let us keep the feast, not with old leaven, neither with the leaven of malice and wickedness [the things of our former lives], but with the unleavened bread of sincerity and truth" (vv. 7*b*-8). Every Jewish person who read that would know what Paul was talking about. What did he mean by saying that Christ is our passover?

(*b*) In relation to separation

In Exodus 12, God tells the Israelites that He is going to release them from their four-hundred-year captivity in Egypt. He tells them that before they left, they are to have a Passover feast. They are to put the blood of a lamb on their doorposts so that when the angel of death comes by their homs, they will be safe (vv. 3-13). When the angel sees the blood on the doorposts of an Israelite's home, he will pass over that home. God then commands them to keep the Passover Feast to remember the time when He passed over their homes and mercifully spared them.

When the Israelites celebrated the Passover Feast, they used unleavened bread. Because the Feast was celebrated over a period of seven days, they had unleavened bread for seven days. Why? Exodus 12:39 says that it was symbolic of their having to leave Egypt in haste. But it was also symbolic in the same way that it is in 1 Corinthians 5. God was saying, "You're leaving Egypt. You are a new people going to the Promised Land. Therefore, don't make leavened bread, because if you do, the leaven is going to come from the bread you made when you were in Egypt."

Unleavened bread symbolized the Israelites' disconnection from Egypt. After the seventh day of the Passover Feast, they were allowed to make leavened bread again. In Leviticus 23:15–21, God tells them to offer leavened bread to Him. If leaven were symbolic of sinfulness, then God would not have had them offer leavened bread to Him. He wouldn't have limited the making of unleavened bread to the seven-day Passover period. If leaven were symbolic of evil, then the Israelites went through the rest of their lives demonstrating God's tolerance for evil every time they made bread.

The only reason the Israelites cut off the leavening process was to symbolize that they were starting all over again with no Egyptian influence. They had a hard time letting go of Egypt too. Once they got out in the wilderness, they started complaining, "We remember the fish which we did eat in Egypt freely . . . and the leeks, and the onions, and the garlic" (Num. 11:5). They wanted to go back to Egypt to enjoy all the provisions they had received there. But the Lord wanted them to cut the cord with Egypt.

Now we can understand what Paul means in 1 Corinthians 5. He's saying that, in a spiritual sense, Christ is our Passover—He has delivered us. Now that we have been delivered out of our old life into a new life, we are not to use any of the leaven from our old life. Thus, in 1 Corinthians 5, leaven does not refer to sin itself, rather, it refers to the permeating influences that come from our past life.

The Jewish Perspective of Leaven

Jewish rabbis used to talk about the fact that leaven was not necessarily negative, but could be used in a positive sense. One rabbi said, "Great is peace in that peace is to the earth as is the leaven to the dough" (William Barclay, *And Jesus Said* [Philadelphia: Westminster, 1970], p. 61). Leaven was proverbial and could be used in either a negative or positive sense.

There was an interesting tradition involving leaven. When a Jewish girl was getting married, her mother would give her gifts. One

> of the gifts was a little piece of leaven from the last batch of dough she made before the wedding. The daughter was to start her first loaf of bread in her new marriage with the leaven started from her mother. That symbolized that all the blessedness of the daughter's former family was to be carried on into her new family. The passing on of a righteous seed to the next generation was symbolized in the custom of passing on leaven to the daughter. It speaks of continuity.

    c) The conclusion

The way that leaven is used symbolically in the Bible is very broad. It is an excellent analogy of permeating influence. Our Lord uses leaven to mean that in Matthew 13:33. It is true that leaven is used in the New Testament to speak of evil and its permeating influence, but that doesn't mean that God can't use it to speak of a good influence. He must be using it to mean a good influence because He uses it in one of two parables that show how the kingdom's power extends beyond the influence of evil.

William Arnot has a marvelous and insightful word on this. He said, "Boldly, as a sovereign may, this Teacher seizes a proverb which was current as an exponent of the adversaries' successful strategems, and stamps the metal with the image and superscription of the rightful King. The evil spreads like leaven; you tremble before its stealthy advance and relentless grasp; but be of good cheer, disciples of Jesus, greater is He that is for you than all that are against you; the word of life which has been hidden in the world, hidden in believing hearts, is a leaven too. The unction of the Holy One is more subtle and penetrating and subduing than sin and Satan. Where sin abounded grace shall much more abound" (*The Parables of Our Lord* [London: Nelson, 1869], p. 118).

William Arnot is saying that Jesus knew the disciples understood that leaven was analogous to a permeating influence. They perceived the massive, moving spread of evil, and Jesus spoke to them of something that would convey the unstoppable and penetrating spread of the kingdom—leaven. Jesus was a genius at explaining the spread of the kingdom.

The leaven is the kingdom, and the massive amount of dough is the world that needs the leaven.

The Influence of Christianity

In a sense, Christianity troubles the world. It influences the world for good, but sometimes it's painful for the world to endure. I am reminded of when Ahab met Elijah and said, "Art thou he who troubleth Israel?" (1 Kings 18:17b). The world has always reacted that way to the prophets of God. In Thessalonica, a number of Jewish people said of Paul and Silas, "These that have turned the world upside down are come here also" (Acts 17:6b). Paul and Silas were accused of disturbing the city of Philippi (Acts 16:20). Christians have been disturbing people for two thousand years with incredible results. From a start of about 120 disciples banded together in Jerusalem (Acts 1:15), millions of people across the face of the earth have been influenced by Christianity. Social advances, legal systems, welfare, education, art, music, and many other things reflect the influence of Christianity. Most of the benevolent societies that help the poor and aid those that are downtrodden and depressed come out of the Spirit of Christ in the hearts of His people, who are leaven in the world. Notice how people are treated in the countries of the world that have never been touched by Christianity. The world has been leavened and influenced dramatically.

What a parable of hope for the discouraged disciples, who had expected the Lord to bring the kingdom immediately! They were worried about what evil would do to their little group, but Jesus said, "You're like leaven, and you're going to bubble and foment and eventually permeate the whole world."

Let's look, now, at the second lesson of the parable.

2. The influence of the kingdom comes from within

The positive influence of the kingdom comes from within the world. God planted His leaven inside the world. The reason He is letting the tares grow with the wheat is so that we can influence the tares. This is the time for Christianity to do its work and reach out for men to be saved. You can think of it this way: The world has been injected with eternal life that is spreading. The tiny piece of leaven that was planted in the incarnation—the little babe in Bethlehem—will someday dominate the world. Ultimately, every knee will bow to Christ. We are extensions of Christ—He dwells in us. The life I live, I live by the faith of the Son of God who loved me and gave Himself for me. It is not I who lives, but Christ living in me (Gal. 2:20). The life of Christ leavens the world through Christians, and His influence permeates the world more and more. We don't need to be politicians, presidents, or have the government help us to influence the world. We don't have to make laws and have guns and soldiers help us dominate the world with Christianity.

In Matthew 24:14, the Bible says that before the Lord returns, "this gospel of the kingdom shall be preached in all the world for a witness unto all nations." It's going to permeate everything. After that happens, the Lord will finally come and set up His kingdom.

Conclusion

A. The Statistics

Do you know where Christianity has gone from its small beginning? It's true that not everybody who names the name of Christ is a Christian, but the gospel has spread. There are people hiding in the branches of Christianity, and they are sanctified by the very presence of Christianity in the world (1 Cor. 7:14). The latest statistics indicate that there are more people who call themselves Christians than there are people who belong to any other religion in the world. There are 1.15 billion people in the world who identify themselves as Christians. Islam is second, with 750 million people. Nearly one person out of every three claims to be a Christian. The influence is incredible! It is true that Christianity is distorted here and there, but nonetheless the kingdom has moved throughout the world.

There are eighty thousand Christian missionaries in the world. It is now estimated that there are twenty-five to fifty million Christians that meet in a half a million house churches in Red China. Cuba, despite Castro's communist rule, has forty-six Christian denominations. The church is alive in Cuba.

Some have estimated that there are sixty-three thousand people embracing Christianity each day and sixteen hundred new churches started every week. Do you realize that from the time the church first met in Jerusalem, seven years went by before the first mission church was established in Antioch? Now, ninety-five percent of the people of the world have all or part of the Bible in their own language, and ninety percent of all the tribes on the face of the earth have had the opportunity to hear the gospel of Jesus Christ. Isn't the influence of Christianity amazing?

B. The Specifics

In spite of the weeds, the birds that snatch the seed, and the scorching sun, there is some good soil. In spite of the fact that the world is oversown with darnels, the wheat is growing. In the face of all the evil opposition, the mustard seed grows and the leaven has its influence. That sums up what our Lord says in Matthew 16:18. "I will build my church, and the gates of hell shall not prevail against it." Christ is building His kingdom. The day is coming when it will all climax. "And the seventh angel sounded; and there were great voices in heaven, saying, The kingdom of this world is become the kingdom of our Lord, and of his Christ, and he shall reign forever and ever" (Rev. 11:15).

That is what will happen ultimately. Christianity will win, Jesus will reign, evil will be destroyed, wicked men will be sent to an eternal hell, and the kingdom will come in its eternal fullness. What a parable of hope!

Focusing on the Facts

1. What is the theme of both parables in Matthew 13:31–33 (see p. 83)?
2. Where is the kingdom now? Support your answer with Scripture (see pp. 83-85).
3. What is the message of hope in the third and fourth parables in Matthew 13 (see p. 86)?
4. Describe the way bread was made during Jesus' time. What was the purpose of inserting leaven into the bread (see p. 87)?
5. What size was the "three measures of meal" that the leaven was hidden in? Why was that amount of bread needed (see p. 87)?
6. What evidence indicates that using three measures of meal to make bread was a common recipe (see p. 88)?
7. Describe the differences between unleavened and leavened bread. What two things are true about leaven (see p. 88)?
8. What has to be done to the leaven before it can start its permeating work? Why (see p. 88)?
9. What is the first lesson to be learned from the parable of the leaven? What do the measures of meal represent? What does the leaven represent (see pp. 88-89)?
10. What do some people believe the leaven represents in Matthew 13:33? Explain why that doesn't fit in with the flow of what Jesus is teaching (see p. 89).
11. What does Jesus liken the leaven to in the parable (see p. 89)?
12. What is the argument of those who believe that the leaven in Matthew 13:33 represents evil (see p. 89)?
13. What did Jesus mean for leaven to represent in Luke 12:1? What was the point that Jesus was making (see p. 89)?
14. What is leaven an illustration of? What terms does the Bible use when it is referring to evil (see pp. 89-90)?
15. What should you not do with an analogy? Explain the problem we run into if we say that leaven represents evil (see p. 90).
16. What was Paul telling the Corinthians in 1 Corinthians 5:6? What was he telling them in 1 Corinthians 5:7 (see pp. 90-91)?
17. What kind of bread did the Israelites use when they celebrated the Passover Feast? Why (see pp. 91-92)?

18. Based on what we know about the use of unleavened bread by the Jewish people, what did Paul mean when he said that Christ is our Passover (1 Cor. 5:7; see p. 92)?
19. What did a Jewish mother give to her daughter shortly before the daughter's wedding? What did that gesture symbolize (see pp. 92-93)?
20. Christianity has been a good influence in the world, but sometimes the people of the world react negatively to it. How can you support that fact (see p. 94)?
21. What is the second lesson we can learn from the parable of the leaven? Through what vehicle does Christ leaven the world (see pp. 94-95)?
22. What does Matthew 24:14 say about the influence of the kingdom in the world (see pp. 94-95)?
23. Mention at least three statistics that show the tremendous influence of Christianity in the world (see p. 95).
24. Will the evil in the world overcome the kingdom? Use Scripture to support your answer (see pp. 95-96).

Pondering the Principles

1. According to the parable of the leaven, a small piece of leaven is capable of influencing at least three measures of meal to rise. That is a large amount of dough! Leaven represents the good influence of Christ's kingdom—His gospel and His people—in the world. As a Christian, how much are you allowing Christ to influence the world through your life? Do your moral standards reflect God's teachings in the Bible? Are there some people you know who don't know that you are a Christian? In what ways are you allowing Christ to influence the world through your life now? How would you like Christ to influence the world through your life? Pick one area of your life that you would like to improve and keep track of your growth in that area. Don't give up before you reach your goal!
2. Read 1 Corinthians 5:6-7. How much influence did Paul say a little bit of leaven can have? Have you purged all of the old leaven from your life? Are you holding onto an attitude or action in your life that is sinful? How much influence does that sinful attitude or action have on your life? What kind of influence could that sinful attitude or action have on your brothers and sisters in Christ? Based on those questions, why is it important for you to keep your life pure?
3. The positive influence of the kingdom comes from within the world. The reason God is letting the tares grow with the wheat is so the wheat can influence the tares. How much exposure to non-Christians do you have? How much time do you spend with your non-Christian relatives or friends? Do you spend enough time with two or three non-Christians to be able to be a positive influence in their lives? If you find yourself not spending enough time with your non-Christian relatives or friends,

make a commitment to have better contact with them. Don't make evangelism the sole purpose of your contact with non-Christians, but do make it more possible for them to see Christ in your life and for you to share Christ with them.

Matthew 13:44-46　　　　　　　　　　　　　　　Tape GC 2303

7
Entering the Kingdom

Outline

Introduction

Lesson
I. The Parables
   A. The Parable of the Treasure
      1. The practice
      2. The picture
      3. The principle
   B. The Parable of the Pearl
      1. The pursuit for pearls
      2. The perspective on pearls
         a) In the world
         b) In the Word
II. The Principles
   A. The Kingdom Is Priceless
   B. The Kingdom Is Not Superficially Visible
      1. The worth of the kingdom unrealized
      2. The way to the kingdom unsearched
   C. The Kingdom Is Personally Appropriated
   D. The Kingdom Is the Source of Joy
   E. The Kingdom Is Entered Under Different Circumstances
      1. The stumbling
      2. The searching
   F. The Kingdom Is Made Personal by a Transaction
      1. The character of the transaction
         a) Luke 9:57-62
         b) Matthew 10:37-39
         c) Matthew 16:24
         d) Matthew 19:16, 21
      2. The comprehension of the transaction

Conclusion

Introduction

The topic of the two parables our Lord gives in Matthew 13:44-46 could be entitled "The Incomparable Value of the Kingdom." The great saint

Thomas Guthrie, writing about the value of salvation, said this: "In the blood of Christ to wash out sin's darkest stains, in the grace of God to purify the foulest heart, in peace to calm life's roughest storms, in hopes to cheer guilt's darkest hour, in a courage that defies death and descends calmly into the tomb, in that which makes the poorest rich and without which the richest are poor indeed, the gospel 'has treasures greater far than east or west unfold, and its rewards more precious are than all their stores of gold' " (*The Parables* [London: Alexander Strahan, 1866], p. 213). Our Lord basically says the same thing in Matthew 13:44–46. There is nothing in all the universe to match the priceless value of the kingdom.

Let's look now at the parables, and then we'll look at the principles they teach.

Lesson

I. THE PARABLES

A. The Parable of the Treasure (v. 44)

"Again, the kingdom of heaven is like treasure hidden in a field, which when a man hath found, he hideth, and for joy of it goeth and selleth all that he hath, and buyeth that field."

1. The practice

   Burying one's valuables was a very common practice in our Lord's time. Today, we put our money in a savings and loan, a bank, stocks, bonds, securities, or real estate. But in those days, there were no banks for the common people. Only wealthy people had access to banks, which in those days were not very safe places to keep valuables. It was typical for people to bury anything they had that was of great value. That was especially true of Palestine because it was a place of war. Its history has been filled with battles. In order to keep conquerors from taking their valuables, the people would take them to a field or marked place and bury them, with the intention of recovering them later. The earth was a veritable storage house.

2. The picture

   According to the parable, a man was in a field, and he found treasure there. The parable does not explain why he was in the field; he may have been employed by the owner of the field to work there. He probably came across the treasure while plowing the field. When he found the treasure, he buried it again and sold everything he possessed so he could buy the field and gain the treasure in it. In those days, it was not unusual for someone to find something of value in a field. In Matthew 25:14–30, our Lord tells a story about a man who gave talents (money) to his servants. The first servant was given five talents, and the second was given two talents. They invested those amounts and multiplied their master's money. The third servant, however, buried the one talent given to him in the ground. The master said he should have invested it and received interest on it. The story shows that there were some people who didn't want to invest their money; rather, they preferred to bury it.

Josephus, a first century Jewish historian, speaks of "the gold and the silver and the rest of that most precious furniture which the Jews had and which the owners treasured up underground against the uncertain fortunes of war" (William Barclay, *The Gospel of Matthew*, vol 2 [Philadelphia: Westminster, 1958], pp. 93-94). It wasn't uncommon at that time for a person who was plowing or digging in a field to inadvertently come across a treasure.

3. The principle

There is a question people frequently ask about this parable. How could Jesus tell a story about a man who did something that was wrong? People think that the man behaved unethically by hiding the treasure again and buying the field without telling the owner about the treasure. Let's look at the answer to that question before we get to the main point of the parable.

First, Jewish rabbinic law said that "if a man finds scattered fruit, scattered money . . . these belong to the finder" (William Barclay, *The Gospel of Matthew*, vol. 2 [Philadelphia: Westminster, 1958], pp. 94-95). Because the man who found the treasure was within the bounds of the Jewish rabbinic law, the people listening to the parable would not have perceived the man's actions as unethical.

Second, the treasure that was hidden in the field did not belong to the man who owned the field. If he had owned it, he wouldn't have sold the field without digging up the treasure. He didn't know it was there. Apparently it had belonged to a previous owner, who had probably died in battle or by accident, which prevented him from recovering it. Because the owner of the field didn't own the treasure, the finder of the treasure had prior right to it. Jewish law said that he had the right to claim it.

Third, the man was very fair. If he was not an honest man, he would have taken the treasure and left. He would not have gone through all the trouble of buying the field. You say, "Maybe his conscience bothered him or his father-in-law or another relative told him what he should do."

I thought about something that shows us how honest this man was. He could have taken the treasure, liquidated a portion of it, and used that money to buy the field. But he didn't do that. Even though he knew that Jewish law gave him a right to claim the treasure, he didn't use any of it to purchase the field. Instead, he liquidated everything he owned to buy the field. He knew that was the right way to get the treasure. The man did not do anything unethical—he defrauded no one.

The point of the parable is this: a man found something so valuable that he sold everything he had to get it. He was so ecstatic about finding the treasure that he was willing to do whatever he needed to purchase it.

Let's look at the second parable in Matthew 13:44-46.

B. The Parable of the Pearl (vv. 45-46)

"Again, the kingdom of heaven is like a merchant man, seeking fine pearls, who, when he had found one pearl of great price, went and sold all that he had, and bought it."

1. The pursuit for pearls

The "merchant man" (Gk., *emporos*) was a man who would buy things wholesale and sell them to a retailer. In the parable, he is seeking fine pearls. That was common for entrepreneurs to do in that day—they would be wholesaling pearls and looking for high-quality pearls for themselves. In those days, people who wanted to diversify their investments would invest in them. Pearls were the equivalent of what diamonds are today. They were the most valuable gem in the world at that time. If you owned pearls, you owned a fortune.

Pearl hunting involved great danger. Pearls were found in the Red Sea, the Persian Gulf, and the Indian Ocean. The price to pay in obtaining them was great—many people died while pearl hunting. They did not have the equipment that is available today for pearl diving. Rather, a pearl diver would tie rocks to his body, jump over the side of a little boat, go down into dangerous waters infested with sharks and other creatures and scour the mud below for oysters. A pearl diver had to hold his breath during the whole dive and hope that he wouldn't drown.

2. The perspective on pearls

a) In the world

A pearl that was perfect and beautiful was priceless. The Talmud said that "pearls are beyond price." The Egyptians actually worshiped the pearl, and the Romans copied that practice. When women wanted to show their wealth, they put pearls in their hair (1 Tim. 2:9). The historian Pliny the younger said that the wife of the Roman emperor Caligula, Lollia Paulina, once went to a dinner party with pearls on her hair, ears, neck, and fingers and calculated them at an amount that would be worth approximately $36 million today. He also said that Cleopatra had two pearls that were each worth what would be approximately half a million dollars at that time—money had about twenty times more buying power then than it does now! (*Selections from the History of the World* [Carbondale, Ill.: S. Illinois Univ. Press, 1962], pp. 104-6). When Roman emperors wanted to show how rich they were, they dissolved pearls in vinegar and drank them in their wine.

b) In the Word

Our Lord said in Matthew 7:6 that we are not to cast our pearls before swine. In other words, "Don't give something valuable to a pig; that is a foolish thing to do!" The book of Revelation describes pearls as objects of value and beauty (Rev. 17:4; 18:12, 16) and says that there will be pearls in heaven (Rev. 21:21). Pearls were perceived in those days much the way we perceive diamonds today.

The parable describes a man who went around seeking fine pearls and marketing them to retailers because he could sell them at a profit. Buying pearls was also a good way of diversifying one's investments. One thing a smart investor didn't do (and still doesn't do) was to invest all that he had in one thing. But that is exactly what the two men did in the parables. The first man sold everything he had to buy the field with the treasure, and the second man sold everything he had to buy one pearl.

We've had a chance to learn a little bit about the parables. Next let's look at

II. THE PRINCIPLES

There are six principles we can learn from the parables.

A. The Kingdom Is Priceless

Both parables teach us about the incomparable value of the Lord's kingdom. A person is brought into the kingdom by Christ's gift of salvation. When a person is saved, he will have the knowledge of God through Jesus Christ. He can experience the preciousness of being in the kingdom and the fellowship of the King as His subject. The blessedness of the kingdom is so valuable that a person would have to be a fool not to be willing to sell everything he has to gain it. Nothing comes close in value. Christ and His kingdom are a treasure beyond comparison—incorruptible, undefiled, and eternal. That treasure is lying in the field of this poverty-stricken, accursed world, and is sufficient to eternally enrich every one of the earth's poor, miserable, blind, and naked inhabitants. Salvation, forgiveness, love, joy, peace, virtue, goodness, glory, heaven, and eternal life are all part of that treasure. Both the treasure and the pearl express the value of salvation.

The eternal value of salvation outstrips the value of all the fine pearls in the world or things that might be found in a field. How little the world knows of the gem of salvation! How often the world involves itself in things that are worthless!

B. The Kingdom Is Not Superficially Visible

1. The worth of the kingdom unrealized

The treasure in Matthew 13:44 was hidden. It wasn't lying on the surface of the ground. The merchant had to search for the pearl. In the same way, the value of salvation is not apparent to men. The world looks at Christians and doesn't understand why they worship God. It doesn't understand why a person would want to give his life to Christ and live by a code of ethics that goes against the grain of man's lusts. First Corinthians 2:14 says, "But the natural man receiveth not the things of the Spirit of God; for they are foolishness unto him." Second Corinthians 4:4 says that "the god of this age hath blinded the minds of them who believe not, lest the light of the glorious gospel of Christ, who is the image of God, should shine unto them." The value of the kingdom and the Word are not apparent to men.

In the parable of the pearl, the merchant had to search for the pearl. In the parable of the treasure, the man discovered the treasure and strove to obtain it. But some people never bother to look beyond the surface of things. They are so busy fooling around with the superficial things in life that they never look for hidden treasure. One writer said, "Under the form of man—under the privacy and poverty of a Nazarene, was the fulness of the Godhead hid that day from the wise and prudent of the world. The light was near them, and yet they did not see; the riches of divine grace were brought to their door, and yet they continued poor and miserable." That is true. There have been many times when a Christian would give a description of the treasure or the pearl to a person, only to have that person reject it. Nonbelievers do not understand the inestimable value of salvation. That is why the Lord says in Matthew 7:14, "Narrow is the gate, and hard is the way, which leadeth unto life, and few there be that find it." That is why Jesus says in Matthew 11:12 that the kingdom must be taken by force. It must be pursued.

2. The way to the kingdom unsearched

The kingdom is valuable, but it is also hidden from the people who do not want to look hard for the truth that is hidden in the Word of God. The Lord says in Luke 13:24 that men must "strive to enter in at the narrow gate; for many, I say unto you, will seek to enter in, and shall not be able." That was true of the pearl that the merchant found. Although he didn't have to dig the pearl out of the mud from the bottom of the ocean, a pearl diver had to go through incredible circumstances before he found it. In the two parables we see that, in a sense, the message of salvation is hidden. The world doesn't readily see it.

Jesus says in John 5:40 that some people would not come to Him that they might have life. He tells them to "search the scriptures; for in them ye think ye have eternal life; and they are they which testify of me" (John 5:39). John said of Jesus, "He was in the world, and the world was made by him, and the world knew him not. He came unto his own, and his own received him not" (John 1:10-11). Those who have a superficial outlook on life and do not think of searching for something that is deep and of true value will not find the truth. The truth is not found superficially. There has to be a desire to search for it. The man who found the treasure in the field had to be willing to pursue what he had found.

C. The Kingdom Is Personally Appropriated

That is the crux of the parables. Each man finds something that he personally appropriates. That shows us that you can be under the dominion of God and not be a member of the kingdom. Everyone in the universe is under God's rule, because He is the Sovereign of the universe. Those who are on the earth are, in a sense, in the kingdom. But many of those on earth are not subjects of the King. In the same way, there are many people who associate themselves with the church but are not Christians.

Although the world is under the rule of Jesus Christ, not all of the people in it are a part of His true kingdom. That's why in Matthew 8:12 Jesus says to the Jewish people. "The sons of the kingdom shall be cast out into outer darkness; there shall be weeping and gnashing of teeth." In other words, despite the fact that Jewish people are under God's covenant with Israel, some are never going to personally come to know God. Paul says in Romans 2 that circumcision is not of the flesh but of the heart (vv. 25-29). In Romans 9:6 Paul says, "For they are not all Israel, who are of Israel." The Jewish people are God's covenant people, yet not all are true members of the kingdom.

That is still true today. There are people that are in the kingdom on earth, but have never appropriated the kingdom in their lives. The two parables in Matthew 13:44-46, then, are focusing on the personal appropriation of the kingdom. Before a person can do that, he must come to the point where he sees the value of the kingdom. God has offered something of true value to men, yet people go to incredible extremes to find things that are worthless.

D. The Kingdom Is the Source of Joy

In verse 44, we find that the man's response in finding the treasure is one of joy. He happily sells everything he has to be able to buy the field with the treasure. The basic desire of all human beings is to be happy. You say, "I know some people who love misery." It's true there are some people who seem happy when they're miserable. But realize that if being miserable is what makes them happy, they are still seeking happiness. The world seeks happiness. People want to feel good. The Lord knows that. He says to His disciples in John 15:11, "These things have I spoken unto you, that my joy might remain in you, and that your joy might be full." In 1 John 1:4, John says "These things write we unto you, that your joy may be full." Our Lord says in John 16:24, "Hitherto have ye asked nothing in my name; ask, and ye shall receive, that your joy may be full." Paul says in Romans 14, "For the kingdom of God is . . . righteousness, and peace, and joy in the Holy Spirit" (v. 17). In the benediction in Romans 15:13, Paul says to the Romans, "Now the God of hope fill you with all joy." People want to experience joy. You can find true joy by discovering the kingdom of heaven and the Lord Jesus Christ.

The kingdom is precious and hidden. The person who personally appropriates the kingdom will find the source of true joy. The man who found the treasure sold everything he had to be able to purchase the treasure that gave him joy. There's nothing wrong with that; the Lord wants us to rejoice. The Bible says, "Rejoice in the Lord always; and again I say, Rejoice" (Phil. 4:4). Christians should rejoice more than other people, for they have found treasure.

E. The Kingdom Is Entered Under Different Circumstances

There are some similarities between the two parables in Matthew 13:44-46. Each parable has a man; both men found something of great value; in both cases they recognized that great value and were willing to pay any price to obtain what they had found. There is one big difference between the two parables. In the parable of the treasure, the man made his find by accident. In the parable of the pearl, the man was searching for pearls when he found one of great value. The first man didn't know what he was looking for; the second man did. What does that tell us?

1. The stumbling

The man in the field was not looking for treasure. He was working in the field, possibly plowing it or building something. By working, he was seeking sustenance for his life. In the routine of doing that, he stumbled across a fortune.

There are people who enter the kingdom like that. The apostle Paul was not seeking to enter the kingdom—he thought he was in it. He was on his way to Damascus to kill Christians when God spoke from heaven and redeemed him (Acts 9:1-6). A thirsty Samaritan woman who went to a well to get a drink of water went home redeemed (John 4:7-29, 42). A man who had been born blind and just wanted to be able to see was not only healed, but also redeemed (John 9:1-38). There are some people who go to church to mock the preacher, but then get saved. There are people who aren't looking for the treasure, yet they stumble upon it.

Charles Hadden Spurgeon, when he was young, attended church only because he thought it was the right thing to do. He didn't know Christ and wasn't seeking Him. He was content with his religiosity. When he was fifteen years old, he decided he should go to church on New Year's day. There was a bad blizzard that day, and he could not make it to the church he usually attended. Instead, he went to a small Methodist church nearby. The preacher who was supposed to speak that day never made it because of the weather. One of the church officers went forward and conducted the service before the congregation of about fifteen people. According to Spurgeon, the man was very stupid. He kept reading the same text throughout the service because he had nothing else to say: "Look unto me and be ye saved all the ends of the earth." Then something about young Spurgeon caught the preacher's eye. He said, "Young man, you look very miserable. You will always be miserable in life and miserable in death, unless you obey my text." Then he shouted, "Young man, look to Jesus!" Spurgeon said he looked, and the darkness rolled away; he saw the Son. He hadn't been searching for anything, but he stumbled upon a fortune. Few people have ever lived and affected as many souls as Charles Hadden Spurgeon. That "stupid" man who kept repeating the text to the church had God working through him.

2. The searching

The merchant man knew what he was looking for. He wasn't content with superficiality—he was seeking something of genuine value. He was like the Ethiopian eunuch in Acts 8:26-38, Cornelius in Acts 10:1-8, 30-33, Lydia in Acts 16:14, the Philippian jailer in Acts 16:27-34, and the Bereans in Acts 17:10-12. The merchant man was the kind of person that seeks God—a person that seeks for something of true value. During his search he didn't know that he would find all of what he was looking for in one pearl. He was looking for things that were valuable. He was looking for goodness, honesty, virtue, forgiveness, peace, joy, heaven, salvation, and God. He may have thought he could find them all over the place—in a multitude of pearls. But everything he needed was in one pearl.

So there are people who stumble into the kingdom (from God's viewpoint, the stumbling wasn't accidental), and there are people who search for it. The kingdom is entered under different circumstances.

F. The Kingdom Is Made Personal by a Transaction

In the first parable, the word "buyeth" is used, and in the second parable, the word "bought" is used. Some people get nervous about that and say, "Wait a minute, are those parables saying that a person must buy his salvation?" In a sense, the parables say the men did buy their salvation, but you have to understand what is meant by that. Both the treasure and the pearl were bought with money, according to the parables. But those were only stories. The Bible says you can't buy your salvation with money. Matthew 19:24 says that a rich man can no more buy his way into the kingdom than a camel can go through the eye of a needle. Romans 3:21-26 tells us that salvation is a free gift from God. Ephesians 2:9 says that salvation is "not of works, lest any man should boast."

1. The character of the transaction

Isaiah 55:1 is a great Old Testament passage that talks about salvation by grace. It says, "Ho, every one that thirsteth, come to the waters, and he that hath no money; come, buy and eat; yea, come, buy wine and milk without money and without price." There is a transaction made to purchase salvation, but it's not with money or good works. The transaction is this: You give up all you have for all He has. Let me explain that principle using Scripture, because I don't want it to be misunderstood.

a) Luke 9:57-62

Luke 9:57 says, "And it came to pass that, as they went on the way, a certain man said unto him, Lord, I will follow thee wherever thou goest." The man who came up to Jesus was saying that He wanted to be a follower of Jesus. The Lord said to Him, "Foxes have holes, and birds of the air have nests, but the Son of man hath not where to lay his head" (v. 58). In other words, "Here's the price for following Me: You give Me your comfort and I'll give you My kingdom." The man didn't like those terms, so he didn't make the transaction. Jesus asked another man to follow Him. The man said, "Lord, permit me first to go and bury my father" (v. 59). What's interesting is that the man's father wasn't even dead yet. The man wanted to wait for his inheritance. Jesus said, "Let the dead bury their dead; but go thou and preach the kingdom of God" (v. 60). That man didn't want to give up his inheritance, so he didn't make the transaction. Another man, in verse 61, says, "Lord, I will follow thee; but let me first go bid them farewell, who are at home at my house." Jesus said, "No man, having put his hand to the plough, and looking back, is fit for the kingdom of God" (v. 62). In other words, "You can't plow a straight furrow while looking in the opposite direction." That man was not willing to give up his family.

b) Matthew 10:37-39

The issue is whether a person is willing to give up everything he has to receive Jesus. The Lord says in Matthew 10:37, "He that loveth father or mother more than me, is not worthy of me; and he that loveth son or daughter more than me, is not worthy of me." If you are not willing to give up something that needs to be given up, such as your family, then you're not going to enter the kingdom. Continuing on, Jesus said, "And he that taketh not his cross and followeth after me, is not worthy of me. He that findeth his life shall lose it; and he that loseth his life for my sake shall find it" (vv. 38-39). That's the transaction. You give up all that you are and receive all that He is. That's how one receives salvation.

c) Matthew 16:24

In Matthew 16:24, Jesus says to His disciples, "If any man will come after me, let him deny himself, and take up his cross, and follow me." The basic principle in salvation is that a person gives himself up to make Christ the ruler of his life.

d) Matthew 19:16, 21

In Matthew 19, a rich young ruler comes to Jesus and says, "What good thing shall I do, that I may have eternal life?" (v. 16). Jesus said, "If thou wilt be perfect, go and sell what thou hast, and give to the poor, and thou shalt have treasure in heaven; and come and follow me" (v. 21). Jesus was saying, "If you want My treasure, then give away all of yours." He wasn't saying that if the rich man gave all his money to the poor, he would be saved. A person becomes saved when he is willing to abandon everything he has to affirm that Christ is the Lord of his life. A person must exchange his sin and self-will for Christ's leadership.

2. The comprehension of the transaction

I don't think everyone completely understands that principle at the moment of his salvation, but true salvation is marked by a willingness to give up one's self. A person doesn't become saved by stopping his sinning. cursing, drinking, wife beating, arguing, fighting, and lusting before coming to Christ. A person can't get rid of all of those things by himself. A person becomes saved when he exchanges his will and resources for Christ's strength and power. That's the transaction—a willingness to abandon everything for Christ's lordship.

There is an illustration of this in Philippians 3. There Paul lists the things that had once given him confidence in his flesh—the things he felt gave him the right to be saved. "[I was] circumcised the eighth day, of the stock of Israel, of the tribe of Benjamin, an Hebrew of the Hebrews; as touching the law, a Pharisee; concerning zeal, persecuting the church; touching the righteousness which is in the law, blameless" (vv. 5–6). Paul had been proud that he was Jewish and self-righteous. But when he was confronted by Christ, he said, "What things were gain to me, those I counted loss for Christ" (v. 7). Paul literally said, "I consider all the works of my flesh to be dung (manure), that I may gain Christ." He was like the man buying the treasure and the merchant buying the pearl because he liquidated all of his self-righteousness, resources, and self-will for the lordship of Jesus Christ. Paul may not have understood all of the implications of what he said, but he was willing to give himself up for Christ. Paul said that any price was worth sacrificing just to be found in Christ (v. 9), to know Him (v. 10), and to attain the resurrection of the dead (v. 11).

I think that when people present the gospel, they don't stress enough the cost of following Christ. We are to call sinners to make a transaction. Jesus says in Luke 14:28, "For which of you, intending to build a tower, sitteth not down first, and counteth the cost, whether he has sufficient to finish it?" He adds in verse 31, "Or what king, going to make war against another king, sitteth not down first, and consulteth whether he is able with ten thousand to meet him that cometh against him with twenty thousand?" A person must realize that there is a cost to following Christ. It's worth it, though. The treasure and the pearl were both worth everything their purchasers owned; following Christ is worth any cost.

Conclusion

I once read a story to my daughter about a caterpillar named Stripe. He became bored with just crawling around in a field. One day, when he was looking off in the distance, he saw a pillar going up into the sky. He thought, "I wonder what that is." He crawled toward the pillar and saw that it was a pillar of caterpillars climbing upward. He couldn't see the top of the pillar because it went up into a cloud. He thought, "Maybe that's what caterpillars are supposed to do—climb caterpillar pillars." He got on the caterpillar pillar and started to climb up. The only way to do that was to step on other caterpillars' heads, so he kept pushing his way up. Every once in a while, he would ask another caterpillar, "What is at the top of the pillar?" They all said, "We don't know, but everyone is going up there, so it must be something important."

On his way up, he stepped on the head of a little yellow caterpillar that was very pretty. He felt bad about that and did something someone isn't supposed to do when he is stepping on others' heads—he looked her in the eye. He thought, "She's a lovely little caterpillar." He said to her, "Maybe it would be better not to climb this caterpillar pillar but to go back to the field and just hug a lot." The two of them worked their way down the caterpillar pillar into the field and hugged a lot. After a while, hugging got a little boring, and Stripe said, "I'm going to go back up the caterpillar pillar and see what's up there." She said, "I can't go back up that thing," so Stripe left her.

Lonely, the pretty yellow caterpillar was crawling around in a field when she saw something funny hanging from a branch. It was half of a little case and half of a caterpillar. She said to the caterpillar, "What are you doing?" He said, "I'm spinning a cocoon." She asked, "Why are you doing that?" The caterpillar said, "Because I'm going to die." She said, "Why do you want to die?" He said, "Because if I die, I will be born again as a butterfly." She said, "Are you sure? Suppose you aren't born as a butterfly?" He said, "I will become born again as a butterfly, because that's what caterpillars are made to be. But they have to die first."

She thought about that for a long time, because doing that was a big decision. Finally, she decided she'd be willing to die and be born as a butterfly. She realized that if she did that, she wouldn't have to climb the caterpillar pillar; she could fly over the top and look down to see what was up there. She spun a cocoon and died and was born again as a butterfly. She flew over to the caterpillar pillar and found Stripe very close to the top of the pillar. He was just about to find out what was at the top. Do you know what happened when a caterpillar got to the top? A caterpillar underneath him would push him off, making him fall all the way to the bottom of the pillar and die. But before that happened to Stripe, she rescued him. Later on, Stripe spun a cocoon and became a butterfly too.

What does that story say? It says that if you're willing to die, you can be born again as a Christian. That is the message of the parables of the treasure and the pearl.

The kingdom is precious, hidden, personally appropriated, joyous, and entered from different circumstances. But always the price is to abandon one's self to receive the supreme sovereignty of Jesus Christ.

Focusing on the Facts

1. What could the topic of the two parables in Matthew 13:44–46 be entitled (see p. 99)?
2. Why do some people think that the man in the parable of the treasure was behaving unethically? Give three reasons the man who found the treasure was not behaving unethically (see pp. 100-101).
3. What could the man who found the treasure have done to buy the field? What did he do instead (see p. 101)?
4. Describe what the merchant (Gk., *emporos*) of Matthew 13:45 did for a living. Why did he seek pearls (see p. 102)?
5. What did Jesus mean by saying we are not to cast our pearls before swine (Matt. 7:6)? What does the book of Revelation say about pearls (see p. 103)?
6. What is the first principle we can learn from the parables of the treasure and the pearl? What are some things the text mentions as part of the treasure of the kingdom (see pp. 103-104)?
7. What is the second principle we can learn from the parables of the treasure and the pearl? According to 1 Corinthians 2:14, what does the natural man not understand? Why? According to 2 Corinthians 4:4, what has Satan done to unbelievers (see p. 104)?
8. Why do some people never bother to look beyond the surface of things (see pp. 104-105)?
9. The truth is not found _____. What attitude must a person have to find the truth (see p. 105)?
10. What is the third principle we can learn from the parables of the treasure and the pearl? Explain the truth Jesus taught to the Jewish people in Matthew 8:12. Is the principle taught in Matthew 8:12 only applicable to Jewish people? Explain (see pp. 105-106).
11. What must a person do before he can personally appropriate the kingdom (see p. 106)?
12. What is the basic desire of all human beings? How can that desire be fulfilled (see p. 106)?
13. What are the similarities between the two parables in Matthew 13:44–46? What is the difference between them (see p. 106)?
14. Mention some of the people in the Bible who came across the kingdom the same way that the man who discovered the treasure did (see p. 107).

15. Mention some of the people in the Bible who came across the kingdom the same way that the merchant who found the pearl of great price did (see p. 107).
16. What will not buy the kingdom of heaven and salvation? Support your answer with Scripture (see p. 108).
17. What was the man in Luke 9:57-58 not willing to give up to follow Jesus? Why did the man in Luke 9:59-60 not want to follow Jesus immediately? What was the man in Luke 9:61-62 not willing to give up (see pp. 108-109)?
18. What must a person be willing to do with everything in his life before he can become a Christian? What kind of exchange must that person make (see p. 110)?
19. List the things that Paul thought would get him to heaven before he was saved (Phil. 3:5-6). What did he consider those things after he became a Christian (see p. 110)?
20. What do some Christians not emphasize enough when they present the gospel (see p. 110)?
21. What is the message of the story about Stripe the caterpillar (see p. 111)?

Pondering the Principles

1. The parables of the treasure and the pearl teach that the Lord's kingdom is priceless. When you became a Christian, you received a treasure beyond price that included salvation, forgiveness, love, joy, peace, virtue, goodness, glory, heaven, and eternal life. How often do you think about the riches that you have in Christ? Do you live your life in such a way that you treasure all that Christ has given you? Read Psalm 119:162. What attitude did the psalmist have toward God's Word? What did he say God's Word was like? How precious is God's Word to you? How precious to you is your prayer time with God and your fellowship time with other believers? The things that God gave you when you become a Christian are the most valuable possessions you have. If there are worldly things that are robbing you of your time to pray, study God's Word, participate in Christian fellowship, and enjoy the things God has given you, then ask the Lord to help you get your priorities right.
2. In the parable of the treasure, the man who found the treasure reacted with joy toward his find. Read Psalm 35:9, 43:4; Isaiah 61:10; Romans 5:11; and Philippians 4:4. Who is the object of the joy expressed in all of those passages? Why did Isaiah rejoice according to Isaiah 61:10? Think of other reasons you should rejoice in the Lord. Give thanks to the Lord now in prayer for all of the reasons you have to rejoice in Him.

3. Read Matthew 16:24. What must a person do before he can follow Christ? When you share about Christ with unbelievers, do you tell them about the cost of following Christ? What could happen if a unbeliever wasn't aware that he needed to surrender his self-will and sin before he could follow Christ? So that you will be prepared to share about the cost of following Christ with those you witness to, memorize Matthew 16:24: "If any man will come after me, let him deny himself, and take up his cross, and follow me."

Matthew 13:46-52   Tape GC 2304

8
The Furnace of Fire

Outline

Introduction
Lesson
I. The Picture
   A. The Catch Collected
      1. With a line and a hook
      2. With a casting net
      3. With a dragnet
   B. The Catch Categorized
II. The Principle
   A. The Focus of the Parable
      1. The time of the separation
      2. The agents of the separation
   B. The Functions of the Parable
III. The Peril
   A. The Discussion of Hell
      1. Matthew 5:22, 29-30
      2. Matthew 8:12
      3. Matthew 11:20-24
      4. Matthew 12:36-37
   B. The Description of Hell
      1. The district of punishment
      2. The details of punishment
      3. The degrees of punishment
      4. The duration of punishment
IV. The Proclamation
   A. The Comprehension of the Message
      1. The remark
      2. The reply
   B. The Conclusion of the Message
      1. The comment
      2. The commission
   C. The Continuation of the Message
   D. The Confinement of the Message

Introduction

Our Lord often spoke about hell; He said many things about the abode of the wicked. Perhaps the most terrifying thing that Jesus ever said about hell was what He told the Jewish religious leaders in Matthew 23:33: "How can ye escape the damnation of hell?" It seems strange for us to hear words like that coming from the mouth of the Lord Jesus Christ, because we don't associate Him with hell as often as we should. He talked more about hell than He did about love. He said more about hell than all the other preachers in the Bible combined. If we were to model our preaching after His, then hell would be a major theme for all of us.

During an interview I saw recently on television, a reporter asked a girl involved in punk rock, "What are you looking forward to?" She said, "I'm looking forward to death." The reporter asked her why. She said, "I want to die so I can go to hell and have fun!"

What deception! Hell is not fun. One writer said, "There is no way to describe hell. Nothing on earth can compare with it. No living person has any real idea of it. No madman in wildest flights of insanity ever beheld its horror. No man in delirium ever pictured a place so utterly terrible as this. No nightmare racing across a fevered mind ever produces a terror to match that of the mildest hell. No murder scene with splashed blood and oozing wound ever suggested a revulsion that could touch the border lands of hell. Let the most gifted writer exhaust his skill in describing this roaring cavern of unending flame, and he would not even brush in fancy the nearest edge of hell."

In Matthew 13:47-50, our Lord tells a parable that warns about hell. In the parables of Matthew 13, the Lord talks about the period of history between His resurrection and return. He is the King, and He rules in the world. He is allowing both good and evil to grow together during this period of time, as we learned from the parable of the wheat and the tares. He is tolerating the evil of this period. But eventually there will be a time of judgment. We have seen the parables that describe the nature of the kingdom, the power of the kingdom, and the personal appropriation of the kingdom. Now we will look at the last parable, which warns of coming judgment. The parable says that in the end, there will be an eternal separation of the damned from the redeemed. Today, over five thousand people in the United States will die and enter eternity, and most of them will go to hell. Let's look at the picture our Lord paints in His warning.

Lesson

I. THE PICTURE (vv. 47-48)
   A. The Catch Collected (v. 47)

"Again, the kingdom of heaven is like a net, that was cast into the sea, and gathered of every kind."

The imagery Jesus gave in the parable helps us to understand what He is teaching. Fishing was a common enterprise in our Lord's time. Some of the disciples were fishermen, so they clearly understood what Jesus was speaking about. Basically, there were three ways to fish at that time. Fishermen still use those methods in Israel today at the Sea of Galilee.

1. With a line and a hook

    In Matthew 17, when Jesus asks Peter to pay taxes for the two of them, He says, "Go thou to the sea, and cast an hook, and take up the fish that first cometh up. And when thou hast opened its mouth, thou shalt find a piece of money; that take, and give unto them for me and thee" (v. 27). In that incident, the line and hook method of fishing was used.

2. With a casting net

    When the Lord comes upon Peter and Andrew in Matthew 4, verse 18 says that they are "casting a net into the sea." A casting net (Gk., *amphiblēstron*) was a very special net. It was circular and had weights on its perimeter. A fisherman would drape the net over his shoulder, walk up to the shore, and throw the net. The net would hit the water as a large, open circle, and the weights on the outside edges would bring the net down over any fish that were in the area. Then the fisherman would pull a cord attached to his wrist that closed the net into a sack and bring his catch up onto the shore.

    The Lord had that net in mind when he called the disciples to be fishers of men (Matt. 4:19). He wanted the disciples to throw out their nets and catch men for Christ.

    The third method of fishing, which the Lord referred to in Matthew 13:47, was

3. With a dragnet

    This is a completely different net, as indicated by the use of the Greek word *sagēnē*. The dragnet is also known as a seine net or trawl net. It is a very large net. Some of those nets covered one-half of a mile. Because of their large size, they could not be used by a man alone. When used, one end of the net was attached to the shoreline, and the other end was attached to a boat. The boat would then go out on the water and stretch open the net. After the net was opened, the boat would begin to move in a circle. Because the top edge of the net had floats and the bottom edge had weights, it moved through the sea like a vertical wall. As the circle was being completed and the boat made its way back to where the net was attached to the shoreline, all the sea life that was inside the circle the boat made was caught inside the walls of that net.

    When the Lord spoke of a casting net, He referred to it in a positive way. He used it as a picture of the disciples catching men for Christ (Matt. 4:19). When He spoke of the dragnet, He was talking about the gathering of men for judgment.

The Lord emphasizes two important things in verse 47—the size of the net was immense and the catch was all-inclusive. The dragnet swept up living and dead creatures, as well as seaweed and other things from the bottom. It caught every form of life that the net encircled.

B. The Catch Categorized (v. 48)

"Which, when it was full, they drew to shore, and sat down, and gathered the good into vessels, but cast the bad away."

That was a very common scene in that day. The fishermen sorting the catch put the good things into vessels. If they were going to transport something, they would keep it alive in a vessel containing water. They threw away the bad things.

Now that we understand the picture, let's look at

II. THE PRINCIPLE (v. 49)

"So shall it be at the end of the age; the angels shall come forth, and separate the wicked from among the righteous."

A. The Focus of the Parable

There are many things we could say about the parable, but the Lord is focusing on one element of it—the separating process that the fishermen went through on the shore. That is a picture of the angels separating the good from the bad at judgment.

During this era in which good and evil coexist, God will tolerate evil. But there is coming a time when He will separate those who are subjects of the King from those who are not. Little by little, imperceptibly and silently, God's net is moving through the seas of time and bringing all men onto the shores of eternity for that inevitable separation. The net draws in all kinds of fish; it is indiscriminating. So, as verse 47 says, the kingdom of heaven is like a net that moves silently through the sea of life. By the time people awaken to what God is doing, they will have already been brought to the shore to be separated.

The only spiritual application the Lord makes from the parable is the separation process on the shore. He does not comment on anything else. I think we too ought to focus on that one thing and learn from the parable what the Lord intended to teach.

1. The time of the separation

Verse 49 says that the separation will "be at the end of the age." The judgment of man will occur when Jesus returns to earth to set up His glorious kingdom. Jesus was not trying to chronologically pinpoint every element of judgment when He said that. He didn't specify whether He meant the great white throne judgment, the separation of the sheep and the goats, or the *bēma* judgment (when believers are rewarded after the rapture). He was just making a general statement that, ultimately, all of the people in the world will be caught in the net of judgment.

2. The agents of the separation

Verse 49 points out that angels will separate the good from the evil. They were also mentioned as the separators in the parable of the wheat and the tares (Matt. 13:41). The Bible makes clear that angels will be the agents of God's judgment (Matt. 24:31; 25:31; Rev. 14:18-19).

God will allow good and evil to coexist in His kingdom for now, but the time of separation is moving closer every day. Jesus also spoke of the separation of believers and unbelievers in Matthew 25, where He says, "When the Son of man shall come in his glory, and all the holy angels with him, then shall he sit upon the throne of his glory. And before him shall be gathered all the nations; and he shall separate them one from another, as a shepherd divideth his sheep from the goats. . . . Then shall the King say unto them on his right hand, Come, ye blessed of my Father, inherit the kingdom prepared for you from the foundation of the world. . . . Then shall he say also unto them on the left hand, Depart from me, ye cursed, into everlasting fire, prepared for the devil and his angels" (vv. 31-32, 34, 41). In John 5:25-29, Jesus says there is coming a resurrection of all men, some "unto the resurrection of life," and some "unto the resurrection of damnation." At that final separation, God will determine an eternal destiny for every soul that has ever lived.

B. The Functions of the Parable

Some people wonder why Jesus taught the parable of the dragnet, which talks about the separation of good and evil, when He already talked about that separation in the parable of the wheat and the tares. One reason He taught it is because the parable of the wheat and the tares emphasizes the coexistence of good and evil, not the separation of good and evil. Another reason Jesus taught the parable of the dragnet is because of His compassion for men. He wanted to warn them about hell. He said, "Watch, therefore; for ye know neither the day nor the hour in which the Son of man cometh" (Matt. 25:13; cf. Mark 13:35). Jesus cautioned people not to take their sins lightly because inevitably, they would be accountable before God. He said that there would come a time when men would live as they did in the days of Noah and that judgment would follow soon after (Luke 17:26-27). Through His prophet John the Baptist, He said He would come to burn the lost "with unquenchable fire" (Matt 3:12).

When Jesus looks at the people around Him in Matthew 9:35-38, He sees a harvest moving toward judgment. His heart was filled with compassion for people on the way to damnation. Jesus showed His compassionate heart for men by warning them of the inevitable separation in the parable of the dragnet.

God does not take pleasure in seeing the wicked die. He is "not willing that any should perish" (2 Pet. 3:9). First Timothy 2:3-4 says that God, our Savior, "will have all men to be saved." Jesus wept over Jerusalem and said, "O Jerusalem, Jerusalem, thou that killest the prophets, and stonest them who are sent unto thee, how often would I have gathered thy children together, even as a hen gathereth her chickens under her wings, and ye would not!" (Matt. 23:37). He also said to the Jewish people, "Ye will not come to me, that ye might have life" (John 5:40). Jesus warned men because He loved them.

The kingdom of heaven is like a net. That net moves through the world unseen. When the net touches the back of a fish, the creature simply swims a little further ahead of it, enjoying what appears to be permanent freedom. Men move about in this world imagining themselves to be free, fulfilling their own desires, with little knowledge that the net of judgment is coming closer and closer. Each time men are touched by the net, they move a little further along. Eventually, they will find themselves hitting the part of the net in front of them. They will make a wild dash to escape, yet find themselves totally surrounded by the net. Finally, they will be dragged onto the shore, flailing as they enter death.

Men may not see God moving in the world, but He is moving. When they are touched by the gospel of Jesus Christ or become scared by the threat of judgment, they dart away into the freedom they think is ahead of them. But sooner or later, they will find they are still caught in the net that is moving them toward judgment. The kingdom will ultimately engulf all men, and God will separate them with His angels.

III. THE PERIL (v. 50)

"And shall cast them into the furnace of fire; there shall be wailing and gnashing of teeth."

That is a horrifying verse. If there were any doctrine in the Bible that could be wished away, it would be doctrine of hell. But hell cannot be eliminated from the Bible. The wicked will be cast "into the furnace of fire"—those are terrifying words from our Lord. He spoke of hell more than anyone else in the Bible and for a good reason. People probably wouldn't listen if anybody else tried to teach about hell. Christ had to be the one who taught about hell. We cannot conceive of eternal damnation. Christ emphasized hell in His preaching. If you don't think that is true, then you haven't paid attention to His ministry.

A. The Discussion of Hell

1. Matthew 5:22, 29-30

   Read what Jesus says about hell in Matthew 5: "Whosoever shall say, Thou fool, shall be in danger of hell fire" (v. 22). He then says in verses 29-30, "If thy right eye offend thee, pluck it out, and cast it from thee; for it is profitable for thee that one of thy members should perish, and not that thy whole body should be cast into hell. And if thy right hand offend thee, cut it off, and cast it from thee; for it is profitable for thee that one of thy members should perish, and not that thy whole body should be cast into hell."

2. Matthew 8:12

   Here He says that "the sons of the kingdom shall be cast out into outer darkness; there shall be weeping and gnashing of teeth."

3. Matthew 11:20-24

   "Then began he to upbraid the cities in which most of his mighty works were done, because they repented not." Jesus condemned people who did not repent of their sin and said they would go to hell (vv. 21-24). Those were serious words from our Lord.

4. Matthew 12:36-37

   Jesus says, "But I say unto you that every idle word that men shall speak, they shall give account of it in the day of judgment. For by thy words thou shalt be justified, and by thy words thou shalt be condemned."

The Lord constantly taught about hell. He talks about it in Matthew 23:14-15, 33; 25:29-30, 41, 46; Mark 9:43-48; Luke 6:24-26; and 12:5. In Luke 16:19-31, Jesus tells a story about a rich man who died and went to hell. The man was in such torment that he screamed for Abraham to send Lazarus with water to cool his tongue (v. 24).

Based on the example of Christ, the emphasis of preaching should be on hell. But people don't do that today. It is convicting that we say so little about hell. The truth about hell is so terrifying and awesome that if the Lord had not taught about hell, we would not believe it existed.

B. The Description of Hell

What is hell? Let me give you four truths about hell that I think will answer that question.

1. The district of punishment

    Hell is a place of unrelieved torment and horrible misery. The Bible defines it as outer darkness (Matt. 8:12; 22:13). It is a place of impenetrable darkness without light. Have you ever been in the darkness of night and longed for daylight, or been in a dark room and wanted light? Darkness will encompass those who will be in hell for eternity; there will be no hope of ever seeing light.

    The Bible also says that hell is a place of fire (Matt. 25:41). The fire in hell isn't like the fire we use to burn something. God uses the word *fire* to describe hell as a place of torment—a place where there will be no relief from suffering. God uses both darkness and fire to describe the torment of the damned.

    The Bible gives us two insights into how people will respond in hell. One is in a parable the Lord tells in Luke 16, where a man who went to hell cries, "Father Abraham, have mercy on me, and send Lazarus, that he may dip the tip of his finger in water, and cool my tongue; for I am tormented in this flame" (v. 24). The other is a statement Jesus frequently made, saying that in hell "there shall be weeping and gnashing of teeth" (Matt. 8:12; 22:13; 24:51; 25:30; Luke 13:28). Hell is not going to be a fun place; it is going to be a place of weeping, screaming, grinding of teeth, and unrelieved torment.

2. The details of punishment

    Hell is a place of unrelieved torment for both body and soul. When an unbeliever dies, his soul leaves the presence of God and goes into hell. His soul probably doesn't go into the lake of fire that all unbelievers will be thrown into after the great white throne judgment—a transcendent body would be required to endure the fire—but it still goes to a place of torment (as was illustrated by the rich man who died and went to hell in Luke 16).

    When an unsaved person dies, his soul descends into hell. In the future, there will be a resurrection of the bodies of the damned, and at that time the condemned will be given transcendent bodies so they can be thrown into the lake of fire. Christians will also be resurrected at that time and be given transcendent, glorified bodies to enable them to live eternally in heaven. Those who are condemned to hell will be raised and given new bodies for the sole purpose of being punished forever in those bodies (John 5:25–29; Rev. 20:11–15). That's why Jesus said, "Fear not them who kill the body . . . but rather fear him who is able to destroy both soul and body in hell" (Matt. 10:28). Some people think that hell will only be experienced by the inner consciousness. But hell will be experienced by the body too. Transcendent, eternal bodies are going to be given to the damned; they will suffer in those bodies forever. The bodies men have now wouldn't be able to endure hell because they would be consumed in a moment.

How do we know that the damned will have eternal bodies in hell? First, the Lord said that hell is a place "where their worm dieth not" (Mark 9:44, 46, 48). When a body is put into a grave, worms begin to consume it. Once the body is consumed, the worms die. But in hell, the worms that consume the bodies will never die because the bodies will never be totally consumed. In other words, the Lord said that the unrelieved torment of the body will go on forever in hell. Second, the Lord described hell as a place where "the fire is not quenched" (Mark 9:44, 46, 48). A fire always dies out when there is nothing to give it fuel. But because the fire in hell will never run out of fuel, it will never die out. Hell will be a place of unrelieved torment for both body and soul.

3. The degrees of punishment

The unrelieved torment in hell will be experienced by different people in varying degrees. Hell will be horrible for everyone there, but some people will suffer more than others. Hebrews 10:29 says, "Of how much sorer punishment, suppose ye, shall he be thought worthy, who hath trodden under foot the Son of God, and hath counted the blood of the covenant . . . an unholy thing." In other words, those who received full knowledge of what Christ did for them but still rejected Him will receive more severe punishment in hell.

In Matthew 11, when Jesus condemned the people in the cities that rejected Him, He said, "It shall be more tolerable for the land of Sodom in the day of judgment, than for thee" (v. 24). Hell won't be tolerable for anyone, but Jesus was saying that it will appear to be more tolerable for the people of Sodom (who hadn't seen Christ's miracles and heard His words) than for those who had witnessed His miracles and heard His words. In a parable about His second coming, Jesus said, "That servant, who knew his lord's will, and prepared not himself, neither did according to his will, shall be beaten with many stripes. But he that knew not, and did commit things worthy of stripes, shall be beaten with few stripes" (Luke 12:47-48*a*).

So hell will be a place of unrelieved torment of body and soul in varying degrees. John Gerstner said, "Hell will have such severe degrees that a sinner were he able would give the whole world if his sins could be one less."

4. The duration of punishment

Hell will be a place of unrelieved torment for body and soul in varying degrees, and it will be endless. The worms there will never die; the fire will never die out; light will never shine there, and the sweet relief of death will never come. The only reason some people are able to endure life with all of its suffering and diseases is because they believe that death will bring relief. But it won't. Because hell is eternal, the people there will go insane. You say, "Are you sure hell is everlasting?" Yes, because Jesus said that the wicked "shall go away into everlasting punishment, but the righteous into life eternal" (Matt. 25:46). Both heaven and hell are eternal.

God never meant hell to be for people. He made it for the devil and his angels. But people choose to go to hell by rejecting Christ. Some souls are suffering that torment right now and have been waiting for their resurrected bodies for thousands of years. But even after they receive their transcendent bodies, they will be no closer to the end of eternal punishment than when they first entered hell. No wonder Jesus had to teach about hell!

The great saint John Bunyan wrote, "In hell thou shalt have none but a company of damned souls, with an innumerable company of devils, to keep company with thee. While thou art in this world, the very thought of the devil's appearing to thee, makes thy flesh to tremble, and thine hair ready to stand upright on thy head. But, oh, what wilt thou do when not only the supposition of the devil's appearing, but the real society of all the devils of hell will be with thee, howling, roaring and screeching in such a hideous manner that thou wilt be even at thy wits' end, and be ready to run stark mad again for anguish and torments. If after ten thousand years, an end should come, there would be comfort. But here is thy misery, here thou must be forever. When thou seest what an innumerable company of howling devils thou art amongst, thou shalt think this again, This is my portion forever. When thou has been in hell so many thousand years as there are stars in the firmament, or drops in the sea, or sands on the seashore, yet thou hast to lie there forever. Oh, this one word ever, how will it torment thy soul!"

Many people are in the net and moving toward that inevitable furnace of fire.

We have seen the picture, the principle, and the peril. Let's look now at

IV. THE PROCLAMATION (vv. 51-52)

A. The Comprehension of the Message

1. The remark (v. 51*a*)

    Jesus asks the disciples in verse 51, "Have ye understood [lit., "put together"] all these things?" He was asking them, "Have you been able to put together in your mind all the information in the parables? Do you understand that in the church age good and evil will coexist, yet the good will continue to grow in its influence? Do you understand that the only way to become a part of the kingdom is to purchase all that Christ is by giving up all that you have? Do you see how in the end, there is an inevitable separation of good and evil?"

2. The reply (v. 51b)

The disciples said, "Yea, Lord," to confirm that they understood all that Jesus had said. I believe Jesus accepted their affirmative answer. Otherwise, He couldn't have said what He did in verse 52. Why did Jesus ask the disciples if they understood Him? In Matthew 9:36–38, Jesus sees the world as a harvest that God would soon judge and says, "Pray ye, therefore, the Lord of the harvest, that he will send forth laborers into his harvest" (v. 38). In Matthew 10, He calls the disciples, and in chapters 11 and 12 He trains them. Here in Matthew 13, He teaches the disciples about the mystery form of the kingdom. Then He asks them in verse 51, "Do you understand what I've said? Are you ready to go out in the harvest and warn people of the coming judgment?" The disciples say, "We understand what you said. We are ready."

B. The Conclusion of the Message

1. The comment (v. 52a)

"Then said he unto them, Therefore, every scribe [Gk., *grammateus*, "learner, teacher, or interpreter of the law"] who is instructed [Gk., *mathēteuō*, "discipled"] concerning the kingdom of heaven."

Jesus had instructed the disciples about the kingdom of heaven. He said to them, "You are now discipled, biblical scholars." That is what a scribe was: a student and interpreter of the Scripture, a theologian, lawyer, and preacher. Some were members of the Sanhedrin. A scribe was an authority on the Old Testament and tradition and was called "rabbi." They were influential. Jesus was saying here that just as the Jewish leaders trained their scribes, He had trained the disciples to become biblical scholars.

2. The commission (v. 52b)

"Is like a man that is an householder, who bringeth forth out of his treasure things new and old."

Jesus trained the disciples to be laborers in the harvest and warn men about the coming judgment. He says here that the disciples are now like a householder who dispenses supplies from his storehouse to meet peoples' needs. If someone needed clothing, food, or care, the householder gave it to him. The householder was also wise enough to dispense both old and new things, so that the old things didn't ultimately become useless. He was a wise steward of everything he possessed.

The disciples were now householders with a storehouse filled with both old and new things. In other words, they knew the Old Testament and knew about the mysteries of the kingdom. Not only could they teach about the Old Testament and Jewish tradition, they could dispense the new mysteries of the kingdom as well. They now knew more than the Jewish scribes. All that the scribes knew was the Old Testament. But the disciples had knowledge of both old and new things in perfect balance. God had called and trained them and now wanted them to spread their knowledge.

The term "bringeth forth" near the end of the verse means "to fling out, or to scatter abroad." Jesus is saying, "You've got all this treasure now, so fling it out." He's telling them to be liberal with the riches they have: "Now that you are trained biblical teachers, give out what God has said in the past and what I have now told you about the kingdom."

Jesus saw men on their way to hell (Matt. 9:36–38). That is why He taught the disciples about the kingdom. He said that good and evil will coexist for a while, but there is coming an inevitable separation and judgment. Jesus wanted the disciples to proclaim that truth.

C. The Continuation of the Message

We are to proclaim the same message the disciples were to proclaim. The people of the world are destined for hell. In Matthew 22, the Lord gives a parable similar to the parable in Matthew 13:47–50. In that parable, a king had a wedding feast. Many people showed up for it. When the king came to see the guests, he saw one man without a wedding garment. (That man was like a fish caught in the dragnet of the kingdom.) The king said, "Friend, how camest thou in here not having a wedding garment?" (v. 12). The man without the wedding garment was speechless. Then the king said to his servants, "Bind him hand and foot . . . and cast him into outer darkness. . . . For many are called, but few are chosen" (vv. 13–14).

The kingdom net will catch many people, but not everyone that is caught will belong to the kingdom. Since we know the mysteries of the kingdom, we have the responsibility to make them known to others. Paul says in 2 Corinthians 5:11, "Knowing, therefore, the terror of the Lord, we persuade men." If we aren't concerned about the fact that people are dying and going to hell, then we are selfish. Christians today seem to have lost their concern for unsaved men.

D. The Confinement of the Message

Recently, a "Christian" broadcasting organization sent me a letter with a list of things that they did not want discussed on their programs. The letter said that they wanted to be a good neighbor to their variety of listeners; therefore, when preparing material for their stations, the following topics were to be omitted: criticism of other religions, conversion, missionaries, believers, unbelievers, the Old Covenant, the New Covenant, the church, the cross, the crucifixion, Calvary, Christ, the blood of Christ, salvation only through Christ, redemption only through Christ, the Son of God, Jehovah, and the Christian life. Then the letter said, "Our listeners are hungering for words of comfort. We ask you to adhere to these restrictions so that God's Word can continue to go forth. Please help us to maintain our position of bringing peace and comfort to those suffering people."

That's not comfort; that's damnation! False comfort damns people. We must tell people the truth.

Focusing on the Facts

1. If we were to use Christ's preaching as an example of how we should preach, what would be one of our major themes (see p. 116)?
2. What does the last parable in Matthew 13 tell us about (see p. 116)?
3. What were the three ways of fishing in Jesus' time? Where in the New Testament do we find examples of the first two kinds of fishing (see p. 117)?
4. What was the casting net a picture of? What was the dragnet a picture of (see pp. 117-118)?
5. What two things did the Lord emphasize in Matthew 13:47 (see p. 118)?
6. What element in the parable of the dragnet did the Lord focus on? What does that element picture (see pp. 118-119)?
7. When will the judgment of man occur? Who will be the agents of God's judgment (Matt. 13:49; see pp. 118-119)?
8. Why did Jesus teach the parable of the dragnet (see p. 119)?
9. How does God feel about seeing the wicked die? Support your answers with Scripture (see p. 120).
10. Describe the darkness of hell. What does the word *fire* mean when it is used to describe hell (see pp. 120-122)?
11. Give two insights into how people will respond to hell. Use Scripture to support your answer (see p. 122).
12. What happens to unbelievers when they die? What will happen to them in the future (see pp. 122-123)?
13. How do we know that the damned will have eternal bodies in hell (see p. 123)?

14. How do we know that there will be different degrees of punishment in hell? Use Scripture to support your answer (see p. 123).
15. How long will people be punished in hell (see pp. 123-124)?
16. What did Jesus ask the disciples in Matthew 13:51*a*? Why did Jesus ask that question (see pp. 124-125)?
17. What was Jesus saying in Matthew 13:52*a*? What does "scribe" mean in that verse (see p. 125)?
18. Now that the disciples were instructed about the kingdom of heaven, what were they like (Matt. 13:52; see pp. 125-126)?
19. What did Jesus mean when he described the disciples as householders with a storehouse filled with old and new things (Matt. 13:52; see p. 126)?
20. What does the term "bringeth forth" imply the disciples were supposed to do with their treasure (Matt. 13:52*b*; see p. 126)?
21. Since we know the mysteries of the kingdom, we have the _____ to make them known to _____ (see p. 126).
22. What does false comfort do? What must we tell others (see p. 127)?

Pondering the Principles

1. When Jesus looked at the world in Matthew 9:36-38, He had compassion toward the multitude of men headed for judgment. What attitude do you have toward the wicked? Although it is right to hate sin, does that free us from the obligation to be compassionate to unbelievers? Jesus came to the world "not to call the righteous, but sinners to repentance" (Mark 2:17*b*). Think of some specific examples of Jesus' compassion for the unsaved. Do you show the same kind of compassion toward unbelievers? Ask God to give you a heart that continually expresses Christlike compassion toward unbelievers, yet still does not overlook the need for sin to be removed from people's lives.

2. The Bible teaches that unsaved people are going to hell (Matt. 25:41) and that hell is eternal (Matt. 25:46). Read John 12:48; Romans 2:3-6; Colossians 3:25; and Revelation 20:12-15. Will anyone escape judgment? We do not know when God's judgment will come upon man; all we know is that it is inevitable. Jesus, not wanting any man to die, knew the importance of letting men know that they could be redeemed. He taught the disciples all they needed to know to carry on His work of calling sinners to repentance. Jesus had a strategy. In Matthew 10, He calls the disciples. In chapters 11 and 12, He trains them. In chapter 13, He tells them about the mystery form of the kingdom and the coming judgment of all men. Then He sends His disciples to preach the message of salvation and to train others to carry out that message. Do you have a strategy for reaching the unsaved people you know? If not, make a list of people you'd like to share the gospel with, then decide how you will go about doing it. Keep those people in prayer. Do you

know how to witness to an unsaved person? If not, ask a knowledgeable Christian or read a good book that explains how to share the gospel with an unsaved person. Find out what verses to use. Make a commitment to memorize those verses.

Scripture Index

Genesis		29:10	6
1:28	7	72:8–11	75
12:2–3	8, 17	78:2	29
Exodus		103:19	6
12:3–13	91	119:18	8
12:39	91	Proverbs	
Leviticus		1:7	38
23:15–21	90, 92	15:5	38-39
Numbers		23:9	39
11:5	92	27:22	39
Deuteronomy		Isaiah	
6:4–7	8	6:9–10	26, 36
Judges		9:7	10
6:19	88	11:1–5, 10	10
1 Samuel		11:1–6	17
1:24		28:11–12	27
1 Kings		43:10, 12	8
18:17	94	54:2–3	76
2 Kings		55:1	108
25:1	84	64:1	28
1 Chronicles		Jeremiah	
2:11	6-7	23:5	84
2 Chronicles		39:1	84
29:30	29	39:2–4	84
Psalms		41:1–2	84
1:3	45	52:12–13	84
2:6–9	10	Ezekiel	
2:8–9	84	31:3–6	78
13:1–2	59	36:26	42
14:1	39	Daniel	
24:1	51	4:10–12, 20–22	77-78
		5:21	51
		7:13	55
		12:2	63
		12:3	64

Joel	
1:19	63
Micah	
1:2-5	84
Zechariah	
8:18-19	84
8:20-23	84
12:10	4
12:10-11	18
13:1	4, 18
14:4, 9	18
Malachi	
4:1	63
Matthew	
3:2	4
3:11-12	52
3:12	63, 120
4:17	4, 10, 27
4:18	117
4:19	117
5:1-12	41
5:22, 29-30	121
5:37	58
6:9, 10	7
6:24	43
6:33	27
7:6	61, 103
7:14	104
7:21-23	59
7:26-27	40
8:12	9, 105, 121, 122
8:14	55
9:35-38	120
9:36-38	125, 126
10:7	4
10:28	6, 122
10:37-39	109
11:12	104
11:20-24	121
11:24	123
11:28	2
12:1	34
12:14	3
12:22	12
12:30	10
12:31-32	2
12:36-37	121
12:46	12
12:50	3
13:1	55
13:1-2	12, 19
13:2	13
13:3	13, 19, 33
13:3-23	21
13:4	34
13:5-6	34
13:7	35
13:8	35
13:9	36
13:10-11	23
13:10-17	36
13:11	11, 17, 23, 69, 85
13:12	24, 38
13:13	25
13:14-15	26, 36
13:16	28, 36
13:17	28
13:18	36
13:19	37-39, 46
13:20	39-40
13:21	40-41, 46
13:22	42-43, 46
13:23	44
13:24	53
13:24-30	21
13:25	53, 58-59
13:26-27	54
13:28	60
13:28-29	54
13:29	60
13:30	54, 62, 63
13:31	71
13:31-32	21
13:31-33	67, 83
13:32	71-74, 79
13:33	21, 87-94
13:34	19
13:35	29
13:36	55
13:37	36, 55
13:38	56

13:39	58-62	4:10–20	36
13:40	62	4:11	5, 52
13:41	119	4:14	37
13:41–42	63	4:33–34	55
13:42	63, 64	4:34	28
13:43	64	9:40	10
13:44	22, 100, 104	9:43–48	63, 121
13:44–46	99-102, 105	9:44, 46, 48	123
13:45–46	22, 102	13:35	119
13:47	117, 118		
13:47–50	22, 116, 126	Luke	
13:48	118	6:24–26	121
13:49	118-119	8:5	34, 38
13:50	120	8:6	34
13:51	28, 124-125	8:9–10	55
13:52	125	8:10	11
16:18	95	8:11	37
16:21–22	68	9:57–62	108-109
16:24	41, 144	12:1	89
16:27	62	12:5	121
17:5	3	12:26–27	123
17:20	74	12:47–48	123
17:27	117	13:24	105
18:15–17	59	13:28	122
19:16, 21	109	14:28, 31	110
19:24	108	16:19–31	121
21:8–9	68	16:24	121
22:12–14	126	17:20–21	74, 85
22:13	122	22:69–70	55-56
23:14–15,121 33	121	24:45	28
23:33	116	John	
23:37	120	1:10–11	105
24:14	94-95	3:30	76
24:31	62, 119	4:7–29, 42	107
24:51	119	5:25–29	119, 122
25:13	120	5:39	105
25:14–30	24, 100	5:40	105
25:29–30, 41, 46	121	8:44	58
25:30	122	9:1–38	107
25:31	119	12:24	69
25:31–32, 34, 41	119	13:26	61
25:41	63, 119, 122	15:2, 6	9, 43
25:46	124	15:5	45
Mark		15:6	63
1:15	10	15:11	106
4:10–11	23, 55	15:13	106

16:13	29	5:9	90
16:24	106	5:22–23	44
16:33	57	**Ephesians**	
17:15	58	2:2	58
Acts		2:9	108
1:6	52, 68	2:10	45
1:7	52	3:5–6	11
1:9	75	**Philippians**	
1:11	52	3:5–7, 9–11	110
1:15	75, 94	4:4	106
7:56	55	**2 Thessalonians**	
8:26–38	107	1:7–9, 10	63
9:1–6	107	**1 Timothy**	
10:1–8, 30–33	107	2:3–4	120
16:14	107	2:9	102
16:20	94	6:9–10	42
16:27–34	107	**2 Timothy**	
17:6	94	2:15	28
17:10–12	107	3:12	41
18:10	61	**Hebrews**	
Romans		10:29	123
1:13	44-45	11:40	28
2:25–29	105	**James**	
2:28, 29	9	1:2–4	57
3:21–26	108	**1 Peter**	
8:22	56	1:10–11	28
9:4–5	25	5:10	42, 57
9:6	9, 105	**2 Peter**	
11:26	4	3:9	120
14:2	72	**1 John**	
14:17	85, 106	1:4	106
1 Corinthians		2:15	43
2:10	28	3:4–24	58
2:14	104	5:19	58
5:6–8	90-91	**Revelation**	
7:14	79, 95	6:9–10	59-60
14:21	14, 27	7:9	4
14:22	27	11:15	76
2 Corinthians		14:15–19	62
4:4	39, 104	14:18–19	119
5:11	126		
11:13–15	60		
Galatians			
2:20	94		

17:4		103	20:7–9		12
18:12, 16		103	20:11–15		122
19:14		62	21:1		8
19:20		63	21:21		103

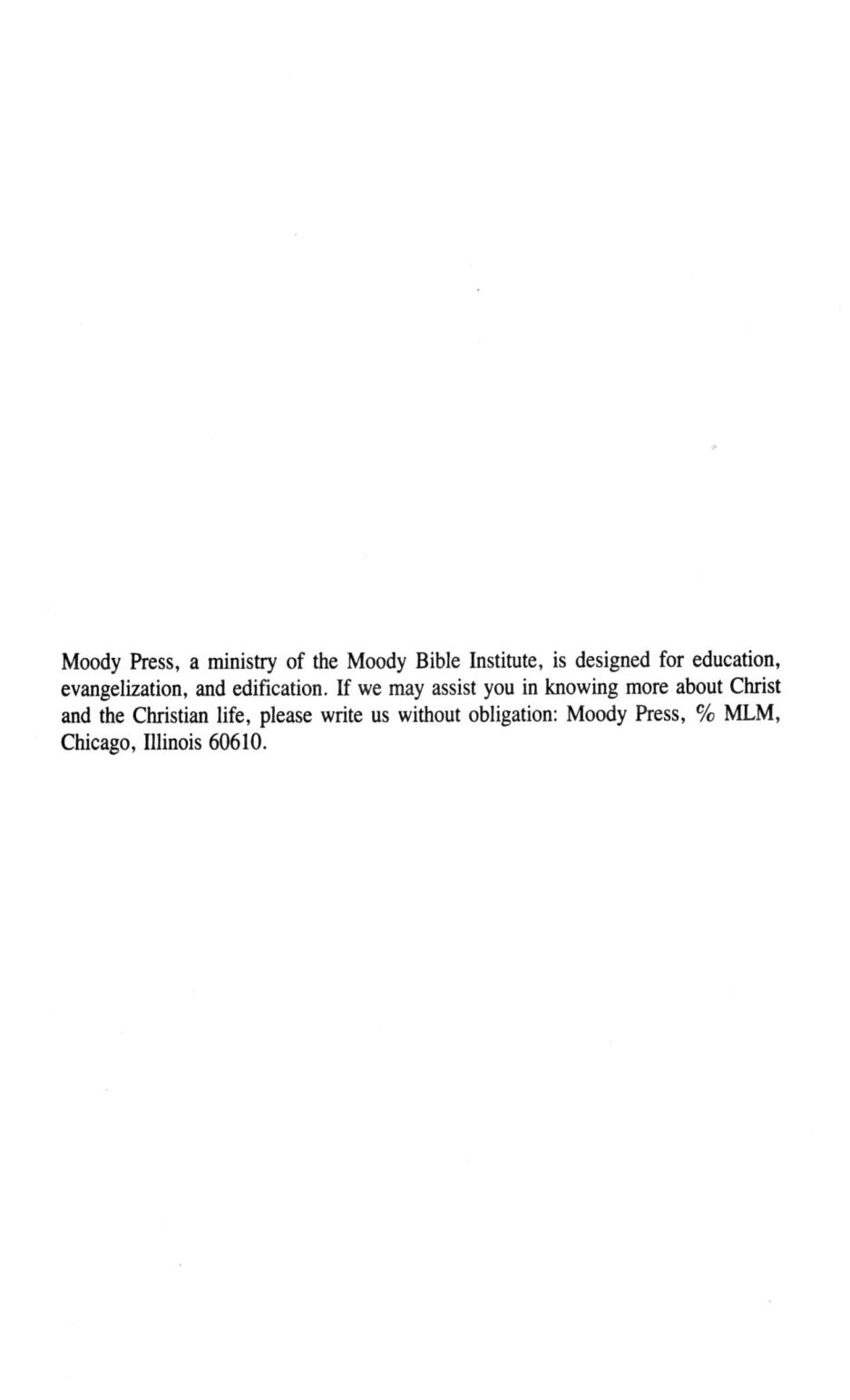

Moody Press, a ministry of the Moody Bible Institute, is designed for education, evangelization, and edification. If we may assist you in knowing more about Christ and the Christian life, please write us without obligation: Moody Press, % MLM, Chicago, Illinois 60610.